**Footprint** Handbook

# Kolkata &
# West Bengal

VANESSA BETTS

# This is
## Kolkata &
## West Bengal

No visit to India is complete without some time spent in West Bengal; this cultured corner of the subcontinent has added immeasurably to India's overall identity.

Kolkata is considered to be the country's cultural hub. Many visitors have preconceived ideas of this oft-maligned city, but a little time spent here is enough for those to be rapidly dispelled and gives a fascinating glimpse into the way more than 15 million people manage to rub along. Travelling north takes you through a fertile land containing such treasures as the terracotta temples at Bishnupur and Murshidabad, the delightful old capital of the Nawabs of Bengal.

Darjeeling is synonymous with tea the world over. Made popular by the British, the hill station has always been a holiday destination, particularly during the summer months, when the cool mountain air provides relief from the heat of the plains. With large Tibetan and Nepali populations, Darjeeling and the region around it have a very different feel from the India of the plains. The monasteries and prayer flags give a taste of the land and peoples that lie deeper within the Himalaya.

If the mountains are too cold, head south from Kolkata to the Sunderbans. A UNESCO World Heritage Site, these mangrove forests are home to a large Bengal tiger population.

*Vanessa Betts*

# Best of
## Kolkata & West
## Bengal

top things to do and see

### ❶ Kolkata

West Bengal's capital is the intellectual heart of India and retains many of its most striking colonial buildings, including the Writers' Building and Victoria Memorial. The spiritual highlight of the year is Durga Puja, when the city is taken over by worship of the clay goddess. Page 26.

## ❷ Sunderbans Tiger Reserve

This UNESCO World Heritage Site is a network of mangrove estuaries sheltering a diverse wildlife population, including the elusive Royal Bengal tiger. You can explore the waterways on a boat-safari, relax in a comfortable lodge and visit local island communities. Page 63.

## ❸ Murshidabad

This magical historic town offers peace and scenic beauty on the banks of the Bhagirathi River. The last capital of independent Bengal, it's dotted with the remains of stunning religious and secular buildings, the most impressive of which is the Hazarduari – the palace of a thousand doors. Page 71.

## ❹ Gaur and Pandua

These two medieval capitals of the Muslim sultanate have gracefully aged into atmospheric ruins. You are unlikely to meet other tourists wandering among the mosques, gateways and mausoleums, and it's a chance to experience local life in nearby towns and villages. Pages 73 and 74.

## ❺ Darjeeling

Bordering Nepal and Sikkim, Darjeeling offers an insight into Buddhist culture and provides dramatic Himalayan views. The nostalgia of colonial-era hotels and riding the Toy Train to Ghoom can be mixed with challenging hikes, whitewater rafting and a cable car ride with views over tea gardens. Page 80.

## ❻ Kalimpong

This little hill station offers a more chilled-out vibe than Darjeeling's hustle and bustle, alongside a wide range of attractive guesthouses and heritage hotels. There are gloriously scenic walks and several colourful Buddhist monasteries on the outskirts of town, and the option of paragliding during peak tourist season. Page 99.

Toy Train at Ghoom

# Route planner

putting it all together

Stretching from the coastal fringes of the Bay of Bengal up to the mighty Himalaya, West Bengal offers travellers a diversity of landscapes, cultures and experiences that's hard to match. Darjeeling district rewards visitors with epic mountain views of Kanchenjunga and Everest, charming retreats among tea estates and an introduction to Buddhist and Nepali cultures. The central plains have exquisite ruined medieval Islamic cities, ornate and ancient terracotta Hindu temples, and the subtle beauty of the rice paddies that swathe the fertile Gangetic delta. India's cultural capital, Kolkata, is rich in colonial architecture and nationalist history, while the southern reaches of the state contain mangrove forests and coastal resorts. Ideally, it requires two weeks to experience what West Bengal has to offer, and if you want to include the Singalila Ridge Trek or a cruise down the Hooghly River (see box, page 13) then it would be wise to add an extra week to your trip.

## One week

Kolkata, Darjeeling and a taste of the Himalaya

With a week's holiday, you can visit West Bengal's two chief points of interest – Kolkata and Darjeeling, at geographically opposite ends of the state – and also fit in a couple of other sights in the eastern Himalaya. This will give a good sense of the contrasts between the humid, densely populated lowlands and the dramatic yet relaxing Himalayan foothills. After flying into **Kolkata** (page 26), you'll need two full days to hit the main city sights and have time to experiment with Bengali cuisine. Visit a couple of key museums, admire colonial architecture, explore vibrant bazars and see temples, churches and synagogues. You can then take the convenient night train to NJP station or a quick flight to Bagdogra airport, both near Siliguri, en route to the eastern Himalaya. First stop in the foothills could be at either **Mirik** (page 95) or **Kurseong** (page 97) for a low-key start to your hill station exploration, from where you can make

Tip...
You'll need at least a couple of days to get to grips with Kolkata, two to three days for a Sunderbans visit, and a week for a trek in the hills around Darjeeling.

Planning your trip Route planner•9

short hikes to viewpoints, tea gardens or Buddhist monasteries around town. **Darjeeling** (page 80) itself has plenty to occupy visitors for two days, including the zoo, a Tibetan Refugee Centre and the cable-car ride. On your second Darjeeling day, take a chance on seeing Kangchenjunga views from **Tiger Hill** at sunrise, before relaxing on the **Toy Train** to Ghoom. Quieter **Kalimpong** (page 99) is a short drive from Darjeeling, where you could squeeze in a day at a colonial-era hotel and visit Buddhist gompas nearby. Alternatively, save your final day for Kolkata, and devote time to shopping and perhaps visiting a couple of the smaller museums and galleries, or riding the trams to explore crowded but atmospheric College Street or Rabindra Sarani.

## Two weeks

wildlife, temples and trekking

With more time, you can maximize on **Kolkata** (page 26) before heading south to the **Sunderbans** (page 63) to spot wildlife and spend a couple of nights relaxing on a boat sailing through the mangrove forests. After returning to Kolkata, you could board a train north to **Murshidabad** (page 71), an old capital of the nawabs. Here you can visit dilapidated mansions, ancient domed mosques and experience small-town Bengali life in a serenely beautiful riverside setting. Alternatively, head to little-visited **Bishnupur** (page 66) to get lost among the laneways and seek out the 17th-century terracotta temples of the Malla kings. Next stop on the road north could be medieval **Gaur** and **Pandua** (page 72), which attract a trickle of visitors to their ruined mosques and Islamic remains on the border with Bangladesh. Catch a train up to Siliguri and either continue straight into the hills or first make a detour east to **Gorumara National Park** (page 76) (closed mid-June to mid-September) to do an elephant safari. With several days left at your disposal, you can make a thorough exploration of the North Bengal hills. **Darjeeling** (page 80) is of course a highlight of the state, but there are also idyllic old-world hotels in which to cosy-up in **Kurseong** (page 97) and **Kalimpong** (page 99). If you haven't made time for the trek to Sandakphu and Phalut, perhaps do as many Bengali tourists do, and take a jeep safari along the **Singalila Ridge** instead (a two-day excursion) to get prime Kangchenjunga views. Rewarding day-hikes can also be made from any of West Bengal's hill stations, including the scenic walk between **Lava** to **Loleygaon** (page 101) in the east.

# When to go

## Climate

It is extremely hot and oppressively humid in the lowlands from April until the monsoon arrives in early June. Inhabitants of steamy Kolkata evacuate en masse to the hills at this time. The monsoon hits between June and September, when large parts of Kolkata are knee-deep in water for hours at a time. It is best to visit Kolkata from October to February, when the weather is much cooler and clearer. October and March to May are also good times to go trekking in the hills. However, heavy storms occur in late March and April, marked by massive cloud formations, strong winds and heavy rain. Occasionally tropical cyclones also strike coastal areas at this time of year, though they are far more common between October and December.

## Festivals

India has a wealth of festivals with many celebrated nationwide, while others are specific to a particular state or community or even a particular temple. Many fall on different dates each year depending on the Hindu lunar calendar so check with the tourist office. If you want to coincide with West Bengal's biggest festival, **Durga Puja**, the dates for the main festivities are: 7-11 October 2016, 26-30 September 2017 and 15-19 October 2018. Local festivals are detailed in the Festivals listings throughout the book. See also page 116.

### Weather Kolkata

| January | February | March | April | May | June |
|---|---|---|---|---|---|
| 26°C | 29°C | 33°C | 36°C | 36°C | 34°C |
| 14°C | 17°C | 22°C | 25°C | 27°C | 27°C |
| 13mm | 27mm | 38mm | 53mm | 92mm | 257mm |

| July | August | September | October | November | December |
|---|---|---|---|---|---|
| 32°C | 32°C | 32°C | 31°C | 29°C | 26°C |
| 26°C | 26°C | 26°C | 24°C | 17°C | 15°C |
| 308mm | 356mm | 283mm | 136mm | 17mm | 7mm |

# What to do

from heritage walks to whitewater rafting

West Bengal has plenty of opportunities for adventure sports. Such thrills can be combined with more conventional sightseeing such as historical and religious sites. Apart from the activities listed here, you can also try paragliding, fishing, motorbike touring, mountaineering and rock climbing.

## Birdwatching

Although not as rich in birding sites as neighbouring Sikkim or Assam, West Bengal still offers visitors the chance to spot oriental species in towns and cities, or more abundantly in the countryside and national parks. On the plains – inside **Gorumara National Park** and nearby **Chapramari Forest** – the cooler months (November to March) are the most comfortable period to see migratory birds from the hills, but the highlands of North Bengal are best between May and June, and again after the monsoons when visibility improves in October and November – most notably in **Singalila National Park**. Water bodies large and small draw visiting waterfowl from other continents during the winter.

For more information, try www.kolkata birds.com or www.orientalbirdclub.org, and www.cloudbirders.com for recent trip reports.

## Cycling

Cycling offers a peaceful and healthy alternative to cars, buses and trains. However, it's not advised to try cycling in Kolkata, given the high levels of pollution alongside hazards posed by both vehicular and pedestrian traffic. Touring on locally hired bicycles is pleasant along the country roads of West Bengal's plains – ideal if you want to see village life – and an option for exploring quieter towns with less chaotic traffic. You should be able to find a bicycle to hire even in small towns – just ask locals to point you in the direction of a rental shop – typically a heavy fixed-gear Hero, Atlas or BSA with a parcel rack on the back. Some places hire by the hour, but taking a bike for the whole day (around Rs 100) is more common.

The steep hills of North Bengal offer an appealing challenge for experienced cycle tourers and mountain bikers, who might choose to bring their own bikes. Multi-day tours that include expert guides, bikes, support vehicle and accommodation (in simple guesthouses

## River cruising

It's possible to take a cruise along the Hooghly River with **Assam Bengal Navigation** – a once-in-a-lifetime experience. Cruises operate all year round, and last between four and 15 days (depending on whether or not you combine a Hooghly cruise with a Ganges river cruise). The beautiful Bengali countryside makes for a mesmerizing view, while land excursions visit villages, colonial towns, and ancient religious and historic sites. Two gorgeous old-style passenger vessels are used: the *ABN Sukapha* has 12 en suite cabins, while *ABN Rajmahal* has 22 and is newer (and more expensive). Both boats are delightfully fitted-out, with a nostalgic saloon bar, the quintessential sundeck and even a small spa.

The seven-day **Historic Hooghly** cruise goes between Kolkata and Farakka, travelling upstream or downstream (with the return journey being made by train) making stops at Murshidabad, Plassey and Gaur. The four-day **Bengal Memories** cruise starts and finishes in Kolkata, and takes in the colonial-era river port towns between the city and Kalna to the north. Ganges cruises go between Farakka and Patna in Bihar, and can be combined with the Hooghly cruises. The company also offers equally delightful trips along the Brahmaputra in Assam, visiting Kaziranga and other national parks. During holiday periods and the cooler months, cabins can be booked out a year in advance, so forward planning is required. Discounts are sometimes offered during the summer months. For more details and itineraries, see www.assambengalnavigation.com.

For a shorter experience on the Hooghly, **Vivada Cruises**, http://vivadacruises.com, offers enjoyable three-hour cruises through Kolkata, either to Belur Math in the north or the Botanical Gardens to the south, with breakfast, lunch or dinner included. **Vivada** also offers a six-day cruise up to Farakka, although its boats lack the charm of ABN's vessels.

or hotels) are best booked in advance through reputable travel agents.

For organized cycle tours see UK-based www.maximumadventure.com and Darjeeling-based www.longwalks.in.

## Heritage walks

In **Kolkata** there are several companies that offer fascinating guided walks taking in the heritage and history of the city, in the company of engaged and informative local guides. Not just visiting the main points of interest, these walks include off-the-radar areas such as markets, food hubs and hard-to-find religious sites. It's an opportunity to gain a deeper understanding of Bengali culture and explore unique aspects of the city. Tours might focus on photography, food or whichever religious festivities coincide with your visit; tours can also be tailor made to suit a client. These heritage walks are best arranged before arrival so you can choose to join with others or book a private excursion. See page 123 for a list of tour operators.

## Trekking

Darjeeling offers a relatively accessible entry point to the eastern Himalaya, where you can view the natural beauty of the mountains, see unique flora and fauna, and meet the hardy people who live and work in the villages and valleys. Any treks described in this book give a flavour of the area and the overall experience, but are for guidance only.

Although it is outstandingly beautiful, the **Singalila Ridge Trek** is not through the icy wilderness that 'trekking in the Himalaya' conjures up. The most popular route follows a rugged, rubbled track that is motorable, and many local tourists will be making this journey by jeep or Land Rover in a few hours rather than a few days. However, it is possible to choose an alternative route to the main trail and avoid much of the vehicular traffic. During Bengali holiday periods the route is, obviously, much busier with traffic.

Trekking permits are not required to visit Singalila National Park; however, it is mandatory to hire a guide for the duration of a visit. Treks can be organized in advance from home or arranged after arrival through a local travel agent in Darjeeling. This will include guide (and porters, if required), transportation and accommodation. Singalila Ridge is one of a few trails in India that offers the ease and comfort of trekking without a tent as it's possible to stay in trekking huts, village homes or guesthouses along the route. Food is simple, usually vegetable curry, rice and dhal.

It is also possible to trek independently, but you still need to hire a guide and pay entrance fees at the entry point to the park. This approach brings you into closer contact with the local population, the limiting factor being the scarcity of accommodation during busy periods. No pre-arranged itinerary has to be followed once inside the Singalila area.

**Deforestation** Do not make open fires and discourage others from making one for you. Limit use of firewood and heated water and use only permitted dead wood. Choose accommodation where kerosene or fuel-efficient wood-burning stoves are used.

**Litter** Remove it. Burn or bury paper and carry away non-degradable litter. If you find other people's litter, remove it too. Pack food in biodegradable containers.

**Plants** Do not take cuttings, seeds and roots – it is illegal in all parts of the Himalaya.

**Water** Keep local water clean. Do not use detergents and pollutants in streams and springs. Where there are no toilets be sure you are at least 30 m away from a water source and bury or cover. Do not allow cooks or porters to throw rubbish in streams and rivers.

## Whitewater rafting

The snow-fed rivers of the Tista and the Rangit originate in Sikkim and flow through North Bengal offering opportunities for whitewater rafting. The rivers range from Grades I-III for amateurs to Grade IV for the experienced. Rafting trips vary from a half-day to two days and allow a chance to see scenery off the beaten track, as well as the option of fishing and camping. The trips can be organized through the **GTA** tourist office in Darjeeling (see page 85) or through a local operator at Teesta Bazaar. The best time for rafting is from December to June; rivers can be dangerous between July and September when the water levels are high.

## Shopping tips

India excels in producing fine crafts at affordable prices through the tradition of passing down of ancestral skills. You can get handicrafts of different states from the government emporia in Kolkata which guarantee quality at fixed prices (no bargaining), but many are poorly displayed, a fact not helped by reluctant and unenthusiastic staff. Private upmarket shops and top hotel arcades offer better quality, choice and service but at a price. Vibrant and colourful local bazars are often a great experience but you must be prepared to bargain.

Bargaining can be fun and quite satisfying but it is important to get an idea of prices at different stalls, before taking the plunge. Some shopkeepers will happily quote twice the actual price to a foreigner showing interest, so you might well start by halving the asking price. On the other hand it would be inappropriate to do the same in an established shop with price tags, though a plea for the 'best price' or a 'special discount' might reap results even here. Remain good humoured throughout. Walking away slowly might be the test to ascertain whether your custom is sought and you are called back.

Taxi/rickshaw drivers and tour guides get a commission when they deliver tourists to certain shops, but prices are invariably inflated. Small private shops can't always be trusted to pack and post your purchases: unless you have a specific recommendation from a person you know, only make such arrangements in government emporia or a large store. Don't enter into any arrangement to help 'export' marble items, jewellery, etc, no matter how lucrative your 'cut' of the profits may sound. Many travellers have been cheated through misuse of credit card account, and left with unwanted goods. Make sure, too, that credit cards are run off just once when making a purchase.

**Warning** Export of certain items is controlled or banned (see page 115).

# ON THE ROAD

## Improve your travel photography

Taking pictures is a highlight for many travellers, yet too often the results turn out to be disappointing. Steve Davey, author of Footprint's *Travel Photography*, sets out his top rules for coming home with pictures you can be proud of.

### Before you go

Don't waste precious travelling time and do your research before you leave. Find out what festivals or events might be happening or which day the weekly market takes place, and search online image sites such as Flickr to see whether places are best shot at the beginning or end of the day, and what vantage points you should consider.

### Get up early

The quality of the light will be better in the few hours after sunrise and again before sunset – especially in the tropics when the sun will be harsh and unforgiving in the middle of the day. Sometimes seeing the sunrise is a part of the whole travel experience: sleep in and you will miss more than just photographs.

### Stop and think

Don't just click away without any thought. Pause for a few seconds before raising the camera and ask yourself what you are trying to show with your photograph. Think about what things you need to include in the frame to convey this meaning. Be prepared to move around your subject to get the best angle. Knowing the point of your picture is the first step to making sure that the person looking at the picture will know it too.

### Compose your picture

Avoid simply dumping your subject in the centre of the frame every time you take a picture. If you compose with it to one side, then your picture can look more balanced. This will also allow you to show a significant background and make the picture more meaningful. A good rule of thumb is to place your subject or any significant detail a third of the way into the frame; facing into the frame not out of it.

This rule also works for landscapes. Compose with the horizon two-thirds of the way up the frame if the foreground is the most interesting part of the picture; one-third of the way up if the sky is more striking.

Don't get hung up with this so-called Rule of Thirds, though. Exaggerate it by pushing your subject out to the edge of the frame if it makes a more interesting picture; or if the sky is dull in a landscape, try cropping with the horizon near the very top of the frame.

### Fill the frame

If you are going to focus on a detail or even a person's face in a close-up portrait, then be bold and make sure that you fill the frame. This is often a case of physically getting in close. You can use a telephoto setting on a zoom lens but this can lead to pictures looking quite flat; moving in close is a lot more fun!

### Interact with people

If you want to shoot evocative portraits then it is vital to approach people and seek permission in some way, even if it is just by smiling at someone. Spend a little time with them and they are likely to relax and look less stiff and formal. Action portraits where people are doing something, or environmental portraits, where they are set against a significant background, are a good way to achieve relaxed portraits. Interacting is a good way to find out more about people and their lives, creating memories as well as photographs.

### Focus carefully

Your camera can focus quicker than you, but it doesn't know which part of the picture you want to be in focus. If your camera is using the centre focus sensor then move the camera so it is over the subject and half press the button, then, holding it down, recompose the picture. This will lock the focus. Take the now correctly focused picture when you are ready.

Another technique for accurate focusing is to move the active sensor over your subject. Some cameras with touch-sensitive screens allow you to do this by simply clicking on the subject.

### Leave light in the sky

Most good night photography is actually taken at dusk when there is some light and colour left in the sky; any lit portions of the picture will balance with the sky and any ambient lighting. There is only a very small window when this will happen, so get into position early, be prepared and keep shooting and reviewing the results. You can take pictures after this time, but avoid shots of tall towers in an inky black sky; crop in close on lit areas to fill the frame.

### Bring it home safely

Digital images are inherently ephemeral: they can be deleted or corrupted in a heartbeat. The good news though is they can be copied just as easily. Wherever you travel, you should have a backup strategy. Cloud backups are popular, but make sure that you will have access to fast enough Wi-Fi. If you use RAW format, then you will need some sort of physical back-up. If you don't travel with a laptop or tablet, then you can buy a backup drive that will copy directly from memory cards.

*Recently updated and available in both digital and print formats, Footprint's Travel Photography by Steve Davey covers everything you need to know about travelling with a camera, including simple post-processing. More information is available at www.footprinttravelguides.com*

# Where to stay

West Bengal has an enormous range of accommodation. You can stay safely and very cheaply by Western standards pretty much everywhere across the state. In the major cities there are also high-quality hotels, offering a full range of facilities; in small centres hotels are much more variable. Hotels in beach resorts and hill stations, because of their location and special appeal, often deviate from the description of our different categories. In the peak season (October to April for most of West Bengal) bookings can be extremely heavy in popular destinations. It is usually possible to book in advance by phone or email, but double check your reservation, and try to arrive as early as possible in the day.

## Hotels

**Price categories** The category codes used in this book are based on the price of a double room excluding taxes. They are not star ratings and individual facilities vary considerably. The most expensive hotels charge in US dollars only. Modest hotels may not have their own restaurant but will often offer 'room service', bringing in food from outside. Many hotels operate a 24-hour checkout system. Make sure that this means that you can stay 24 hours from the time of check-in. Expect to pay more in Kolkata for all categories, except the very bottom rung. Prices away from large cities tend to be lower for comparable hotels.

**Off-season rates** Large reductions are made by hotels in all categories out-of-season in many resorts. Always ask if any discount is available. You may also

## Price codes

| Where to stay | Restaurants |
|---|---|
| $$$$ over US$150 | $$$ over US$12 |
| $$$ US$66-150 | $$ US$6-12 |
| $$ US$30-65 | $ under US$6 |
| $ under US$30 | |
| For a double room in high season, excluding taxes. | For a two-course meal for one person, excluding drinks or service charge. |

request the 10-15% agent's commission to be deducted from your bill if you book direct. Clarify whether the agreed figure includes all taxes.

**Taxes** In general most hotel rooms rated at Rs 1200 or above are subject to a tax of 10%. Many states levy an additional luxury tax of 10-25%, and some hotels add a service charge of 10% on top of this. Taxes are not necessarily payable on meals, so it is worth settling your meals bill separately. Most hotels in the $$ category and above accept payment by credit card. Check your final bill carefully. Visitors have complained of incorrect bills, even in the most expensive hotels. The problem particularly afflicts groups, when last-minute extras appear mysteriously on some guests' bills. Check the evening before departure, and keep all receipts.

**Hotel facilities** You have to be prepared for difficulties which are uncommon in the West. It is best to inspect the room and check that all equipment (air conditioning, TV, water heater, flush) works before checking in at a modest hotel. Many hotels try to wring too many years' service out of their linen, and it's quite common to find sheets that are stained, frayed or riddled with holes. Don't expect any but the more expensive or tourist-savvy hotels to fit a 'top sheet' to the bed.

In some towns power cuts are common, or hot water may be restricted to certain times of day. The largest hotels have their own generators but it is best to carry a good torch.

In a few places water supply is rationed periodically. Keep a bucket filled to use for flushing the toilet during water cuts. Occasionally, tap water may be discoloured due to rusty tanks. During the cold weather and in hill stations, hot water will be available at certain times of the day, sometimes in buckets, but is usually very restricted in quantity. Electric water heaters may provide enough for a shower but not enough to fill a bath tub. For details on drinking water, see page 21.

Hotels close to temples can be very noisy, especially during festivals. Music blares from loudspeakers late at night and from very early in the morning, often making sleep impossible. Mosques call the faithful to prayers at dawn. Some find earplugs helpful.

## Homestays

Increasing numbers of travellers are keen to stay in private homes and guesthouses, opting not to book large hotel chains that keep you at arm's length from a culture. Instead, travellers get home-cooked meals in heritage houses and learn about a country through conversation with often fascinating hosts. Tourist offices have lists of families with more modest homestays.

# Food
# & drink

from grilled *bekti* and smoked *hilsa* to sweet *mishti doi*

## Food

Bengali cuisine is distinctive in both ingredients and flavour from the rest of India. Fish and prawns are common ingredients, especially in Kolkata and the coastal area.

The larger hotels, open to non-residents, often offer buffet lunches with Indian, Western and sometimes Chinese or other international dishes. These can be good value (Rs 300-500; but Rs 750-plus in the top grades) and can provide a welcome, comfortable respite from the heat. The health risks, however, of food kept warm for long periods in metal containers are considerable, especially if turnover at the buffet is slow.

It is essential to be very careful since food hygiene can be poor, flies abound and refrigeration in the hot weather may be inadequate and intermittent because of power cuts. It is best to eat only freshly prepared food by ordering off the menu (especially meat and fish dishes). Avoid salads and cut fruit in places that may have used local tap water for washing purposes. Popular local restaurants are obvious from the number of people eating in them. If you are unused to spicy food, go slow. Food is often spicier when you eat with families or at local places.

Ubiquitous across India is the traditional *thali*, which is a complete meal served on a large stainless steel plate. Several preparations, placed in small bowls, surround the central serving of wholewheat chapati and rice. A vegetarian *thali* would include *dhal* (lentils), two or three curries (which can be quite hot) and crisp poppadums. A variety of pickles are offered – mango and lime are two of the most popular. Pickles and chutneys can be exceptionally hot, and are designed to be taken in minute quantities alongside the main dishes. Plain *dahi* (yoghurt) or *raita* usually acts as a bland 'cooler'. Simple *dhabas* (rustic roadside eateries) are an alternative experience for sampling authentic local dishes.

Many city restaurants offer a choice of so-called European options such as toasted sandwiches (often called "jaffles"), stuffed pancakes, apple pies, fruit crumbles and cheesecakes. Italian favourites (pizzas, pastas) can be very different from what you are used to. Ice creams, on the other hand, can be exceptionally good; there are excellent Indian ones (known as *kulfi*, which is creamier and denser than western ice cream, and served in clay pots or on a stick) as well as some international brands.

India has many delicious tropical fruits. Some are seasonal (eg mangoes, pineapples and lychees), while others (eg bananas, grapes and oranges) are available throughout the year. It is safe to eat the ones you can wash and peel.

## Bengali cuisine

Bengalis are said to be obsessed about what they eat. The men often take a keen interest in buying the most important elements of the day's meal, namely fresh fish. Typically, it is river fish, the most popular being *hilsa* and *bekti* or the widely available shellfish, especially king prawns. *Bekti* is grilled or fried and is tastier than the fried fish of the west as it has often been marinated in mild spices first. The prized smoked *hilsa*, although delicious, has thousands of fine bones. *Maachh* (fish) comes in many forms as *jhol* (in a thin gravy), *jhal* (spicy and hot), *malai* curry (in coconut milk, mildly spiced), *chop* (in a covering of mashed potato and crumbs) or *chingri maachher* cutlet (flattened king prawn 'fillets', crumbed and fried). Bengali cooking uses mustard oil and mustard which grows in abundance, and a subtle mixture of spices.

*Mishti* (sweetmeats) are another distinctive feature. Many are milk based and the famous *sandesh*, *roshogolla*, *roshomalai*, *pantua* and *ledikeni* (named after Lady Canning, the wife of the first Viceroy of India) are prepared with a kind of cottage cheese, in dozens of different textures, shapes, colours and tastes. Pale pinkish brown, *mishti doi*, is an excellent sweet yoghurt eaten as a dessert, typically sold in hand-thrown clay pots.

You will only find the true flavour of Bengali cooking in someone's home or at a few special Bengali restaurants.

## Drink

Drinking water used to be regarded as one of India's biggest hazards. It is still true that water from the tap or a well should never be considered safe to drink since public water supplies are often polluted. Bottled water is widely available although not all bottled water is mineral water; most are simply purified water from an urban supply. Buy from a shop or stall, check the seal carefully and avoid street hawkers. There is growing concern over the mountains of plastic bottles that are collecting and the waste of resources needed to produce them, so travellers are being encouraged to carry their own bottles and take a portable water filter. It is important to use pure water for cleaning teeth.

## Menu reader

### Meat, fish and vegetables
**aloo** potato
**band gobi** cabbage
**begun** aubergine
**bhindi** okra, ladies' fingers
**chingri** prawns
**gajar** carrots
**gosht, mas** meat
**khumbhi** mushroom
**maach** fish
**matar** peas
**murgh** chicken
**phool gobi** cauliflower
**piaz** onion
**sag** spinach

### Styles of cooking
**bharta** roasted then mashed vegetables cooked with spices
**bhoona** in a thick, fairly spicy sauce
**chops** minced meat, fish or vegetables, covered with mashed potato, crumbed and fried
**cutlet** minced meat, fish, vegetables formed into flat rounds or ovals, crumbed and fried (eg prawn cutlet, flattened king prawn)
**dopiaza** with onions (added twice during cooking)
**dum pukht** steam baked
**jhal frazi** spicy, hot sauce with tomatoes and chillies

**jhol** thin gravy (Bengali)
**Kashmiri** cooked with mild spices, ground almonds and yoghurt, often with fruit
**kebab** skewered (or minced and shaped) meat or fish; a dry spicy dish cooked on a fire
**kima** minced meat (usually 'mutton')
**kofta** minced meat or vegetable balls
**korma** in fairly mild rich sauce using cream/yoghurt
**masala** marinated in spices (fairly hot)
**Madras** hot
**makhani** in butter rich sauce
**Mughlai** rich North Indian style
**navratan** curry ('9 jewels') colourful mixed vegetables and fruit in mild sauce
**Peshwari** rich with dried fruit and nuts (northwest Indian)
**tandoori** baked in a tandoor (special clay oven) or one imitating it
**tikka** marinated meat pieces, baked quite dry

### Typical dishes
**aloo gosht** potato and mutton stew
**aloo gobi** dry potato and cauliflower with cumin
**bhindi bhaji** okra fried with onions and mild spices
**dhal makhani** lentils cooked with butter
**kati rolls** rolled up *paratha* with kebab, egg, vegetable or panir inside, with chilli sauce and onions

Tea and coffee are safe and widely available. Both are normally served sweet, and with milk. If you wish, say 'no sugar' (*chini nahin*) or 'no milk' (*dudh nahin*) when ordering. Alternatively, in a hotel you can ask for a pot of tea and milk and sugar to be brought separately. Freshly brewed coffee is uncommon in northern India and ordinary city restaurants will usually serve the instant variety. Even in aspiring smart cafés, espresso or cappuccino may not turn out quite as you'd expect in the West.

Bottled soft drinks such as Coke, Pepsi, Limca and Thums Up are universally available but always check the seal when you buy from a street stall. There are also several brands of fruit juice sold in cartons, including mango, pineapple and apple – Indian brands are very sweet. Don't add ice cubes as the water source may be contaminated. Take care with fresh fruit juices or *lassis* (delicious yoghurt-based drinks) as ice is often added.

**matar panir** curd cheese cubes with peas and spices (and often tomatoes)

**rogan josh** rich, mutton/beef pieces in creamy, red sauce

**sag panir** drained curd (*panir*) sautéd with chopped spinach in mild spices

## Rice

**bhaat chawal** plain boiled rice

**biriyani** partially cooked rice layered over meat and baked with saffron

**khichari** rice and lentils cooked with turmeric and other spices

**pulao/pilau** fried rice cooked with spices and dried fruit, nuts or vegetables. Sometimes cooked with meat, like a biriyani

## Roti – breads

**chapati (roti)** thin, plain, wholemeal unleavened bread cooked on a *tawa* (griddle), usually made from *ata* (wheat flour)

**naan** oven baked (traditionally in a tandoor) white flour leavened bread often large and triangular

**paratha** fried bread layered with *ghi* (sometimes cooked with egg or with potatoes)

**poori** thin deep-fried, puffed rounds of flour

## Sweets

These are often made with reduced/thickened milk, drained curd cheese or powdered lentils and nuts. They are sometimes covered with a flimsy sheet of decorative, edible silver leaf.

**barfi** fudge-like rectangles/diamonds

**gulab jamun** dark fried spongy balls, soaked in syrup

**khir, payasam, paesh** thickened milk rice/vermicelli pudding

**kulfi** cone-shaped Indian ice cream with pistachios/almonds, uneven in texture

**jalebi** spirals of fried batter soaked in syrup

**laddoo** lentil-based batter 'grains' shaped into rounds

**rasgulla (roshgulla)** balls of curd in clear syrup

**sandesh** dry sweet made of curd cheese

## Snacks

**bhaji, pakora** vegetable fritters (onions, potatoes, cauliflower, etc) deep-fried in batter

**chat** sweet and sour fruit and vegetables flavoured with tamarind paste and chillies

**chana choor, chioora ('Bombay mix')** lentil and flattened rice snacks mixed with nuts and dried fruit

**dosai** South Indian pancake made with rice and lentil flour; served with a mild potato and onion filling (*masala dosai*) or without (plain *dosai*)

**idli** steamed South Indian rice cakes, a bland breakfast given flavour by spiced accompaniments

**kachori** fried pastry rounds stuffed with spiced lentil/peas/potato filling

**samosa** cooked vegetable or meat wrapped in pastry triangles and deep fried

**vadai** deep fried, small savoury lentil 'doughnut' rings. *Dahi vada* are similar rounds in yoghurt

Indians rarely drink alcohol with a meal. In the past wines and spirits were generally either imported and extremely expensive, or local and of poor quality. Now, the best Indian whisky, rum and brandy (IMFL or 'Indian Made Foreign Liquor') are widely accepted, as are good Champagnoise and other wines from Maharashtra. If you hanker after a bottle of imported wine, you will only find it in the top restaurants for at least Rs 1000. For the urban elite, refreshing Indian beers are popular when eating out and are widely available. 'Pubs' have sprung up in the major cities. Elsewhere, seedy, all-male drinking dens in the larger cities are best avoided for women travellers, but can make quite an experience otherwise – you will sometimes be locked into cubicles for clandestine drinking. If that sounds unsavoury then head for the better hotel bars instead. The legal drinking age in West Bengal is 21, and the state forces 'dry days' during some festivals and national holidays.

# Kolkata &
## West Bengal

To Bengalis Kolkata is the proud intellectual capital of India, with an outstanding contribution to the arts, medicine and social reform in its past, and a rich contemporary cultural life. As the former imperial capital, Kolkata retains some of the country's most striking colonial buildings, yet at the same time it is truly an Indian city. It is unique in India in retaining trams and is the only place in the world to still have hand-pulled rickshaws — you take your life in your hands each time you cross Kolkata's streets. Kolkata's Maidan, the parkland, are the lungs of a city that is packed with some of the most densely populated slums, or bustees, anywhere in the world.

Most of West Bengal lies on the western delta of the Ganga. The flat landscape of the Bengali plains is given variety by the contrasting greens of the rice paddies; higher ground is limited to the Rajmahal Hills just west of Murshidabad. In the north, however, are the southern slopes of the Himalaya which provide far greater scenic contrasts, including remains of the dense forests that once covered the state. In the far south are the mangrove swamps of the Sunderbans.

# Kolkata (Calcutta)

memories of the British in India

## BBD Bagh (Dalhousie Square) and around

Many historic Raj buildings surround the square, which is quietest before 0900. Renamed Benoy Badal Dinesh (BBD) Bagh after three Bengali martyrs, the square has an artificial lake (tank) fed by natural springs that used to supply water to Kolkata's first residents.

The **Writers' Building** (1780), designed by Thomas Lyon as the trading headquarters of the East India Company, was refaced in 1880. It is now the state Government Secretariat. The classical block with 57 sets of identical windows was built like barracks inside. Across the road to the east, elegant **St Andrew's Kirk** (1814) ① *0900-1400*, like the earlier St John's Church (1787), was modelled partially on St Martin-in-the-Fields, London.

On the west side of the square, the white domed **General Post Office** (1866) was built on the site of the first Fort William. Around the corner, there is a quaint little **Postal Museum** ① *Mon-Sat 1100-1600, free*, which displays shabby maps, original post boxes and has a philatelic library.

Running along the south of the square, **Mission Row** (now RN Mukherjee Road) is Kolkata's oldest street, and contains the **Old Mission Church** (consecrated 1770), built by the Swedish missionary Johann Kiernander.

**Metcalfe Hall** ① *Strand Rd, entrance from rear. Mon-Sat 1000-1700.* Facing the Hooghly (also spelt Hugli) on Strand Road is colonnaded **Metcalfe Hall** modelled on the Palace of Winds in Athens. This was once the home of the Imperial Library, and still contains the journals of the Asiatic Society in the ground floor **library** ① *Mon-Fri 0945-1815 (allegedly)*, plus a small exhibition on the first floor including glazed tiles from Gaur and Pandua, and a gallery of bricks. Unsurprisingly, the visitors' book shows an average of two tourists per month.

**St John's Church** ① *Council House St, 0800-1700, Rs 10.* The church was built in 1787 on soft subsoil that did not allow it to have a tall spire, and architecturally it was thought to be 'full of blunders'. Verandas were added to the north and south in 1811 to reduce the glare of the sun. Inside the vestry are Warren Hastings's table and chair, plus Raj-era paintings and prints. *The Last Supper*, by Johann Zoffany was restored in 2010 and shows the city's residents dressed as the apostles. Job Charnock is buried in the grounds. His octagonal mausoleum, the oldest piece of masonry in the city, is of Pallavaram granite (from Madras Presidency), which is named charnockite after him. The memorial built by Lord Curzon to the **Black Hole of Calcutta** was brought here from Dalhousie Square (BBD Bagh) in 1940.

**Raj Bhavan** Directly south of BBD Bagh is the imposing Raj Bhavan (1799-1802), the residence of the Governor of West Bengal, formerly Government House. It was modelled on Kedleston Hall in Derbyshire, England (later Lord Curzon's home), and designed by Charles Wyatt, one of many Bengal engineers who based their designs on famous British buildings

# Essential Kolkata

## Finding your feet

Subhas Chandra Bose Airport at Dum Dum has an 'integrated terminal' for domestic and international flights, which opened in 2013. Transport to the city centre is by taxi or bus. Arrival at Howrah Train Station, on the west bank of the Hooghly, can be daunting and the taxi rank outside is often chaotic; use the prepaid taxi booth to the right as you exit – check the price chart and note that Sudder Street is less than 5 km. Trains to/from the north use the slightly less chaotic Sealdah Terminal east of the centre, which also has prepaid taxis. Long-distance buses arrive at Esplanade, 15 minutes' walk from most budget hotels. For further details, see Transport, page 60.

## Warning...

Asthma sufferers will find the traffic pollution in Kolkata very trying.

## Getting around

You can cover much of Central Kolkata on foot. You may not fancy using hand-pulled rickshaws, but they become indispensable (and more costly) when the streets are

## Best Kolkata watering holes

**Indian Coffee House**, page 50
**Flury's**, page 51
**Blue & Beyond**, page 54
**Broadway Bar**, page 54
**Fairlawn Hotel**, page 54
**Oly Pub**, page 54

flooded during monsoons. Buses and minibuses are often jam-packed, but routes comprehensively cover the city – conductors and bystanders will help you find the correct bus. The electric trams are slow but they are incredibly cheap and cover some interesting routes. The Metro, though limited to one line and very crowded, is the easiest way of getting from north to south. Taxis are relatively cheap (note that the meter reading is not the true fare; expect to pay double the meter fare, based on the driver's conversion chart), but you should allow plenty of time to get through very congested traffic. Many city centre roads become one-way or change direction from 1400 to 2100, so expect tortuous detours. Despite the footpath, it is not permitted to walk across the Vidyasagar Bridge (taxi drivers expect passengers to pay the Rs 10 toll). For further details, see Transport, page 60.

(entrance not permitted). Nearby, the **Great Eastern Hotel** (1841) was in Mark Twain's day "the best hotel East of the Suez", but from the 1970s it steadily declined. However, it recently underwent major restoration by the Lalit group of hotels and reopened in 2014.

**Kolkata Panorama** ⓘ *Tue-Sun 1100-1800, last entry 1700, foreigners Rs 10 (Rs 15 on Sat), bag deposit*. The beautiful old **Town Hall** (1813) has been converted into a museum, telling the story of the independence movement in Bengal through a panoramic, cinematic display, starring an animatronic Rabindranath Tagore. Visitors are sped through in grouped tours, however, and some of the videos drag on rather. There's a good life-size diorama of a Bengali street and some great film posters.

**High Court** The bright-red gothic High Court (1872) was modelled on the medieval cloth merchants' hall at Ypres in Flanders. It is possible to enter through Gate F: a fascinating

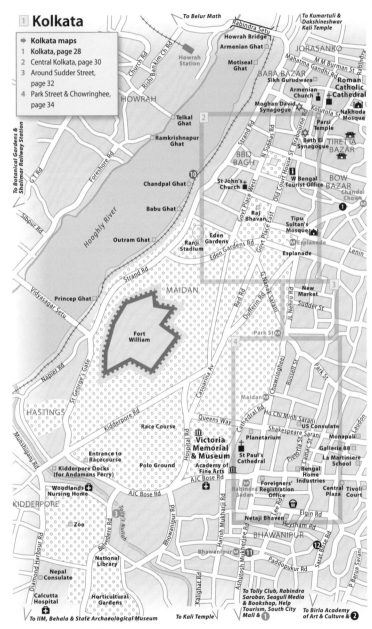

# Kolkata

➡ Kolkata maps
1 Kolkata, page 28
2 Central Kolkata, page 30
3 Around Sudder Street, page 32
4 Park Street & Chowringhee, page 34

To Belur Math

To Kumartuli & Dakshineshwar Kali Temple

Rabindra Setu

Howrah Bridge

Armenian Ghat

JORASANKO

M M Burman St

Mahatma Gandhi Rd

Motiseal Ghat

BARA BAZAR

Sikh Gurudwara

Roman Catholic Cathedral

Howrah Station

Rishi Bankim Ch Rd

Church Rd

HOWRAH

Armenian Church

Moghan David Synagogue

Kolutola Rd

Nakhoda Mosque

Parsi Temple

TIRETTA BAZAR

Telkal Ghat

Beth El Synagogue

BBD BAGH

BOW BAZAR

Ramkrishnapur Ghat

Strand Rd

N Subhas Rd

Brabourne Rd

Old Court House St

Chandni Chowk

Chandpal Ghat

St John's Church

W Bengal Tourist Office

Babu Ghat

Raj Bhavan

Tipu Sultan's Mosque

Govt Place West

Govt Place East

Eden Gardens

Esplanade

Esplanade

Lenin

Outram Ghat

Ranji Stadium

Eden Gardens Rd

To Botanical Gardens & Shalimar Railway Station

Foreshore Rd

GT Rd

Sibpur Rd

Hooghly River

Strand Rd

MAIDAN

Red Rd

Chittaranjan Rd

New Market

Sudder St

Princep Ghat

Vidyasagar Setu

Dufferin Rd

JL Nehru Rd

Park St

Park St

Fort William

St George's Gate

Napier Rd

HASTINGS

Kidderpore Rd

Casuarina Av

Queens Way

Maidan

Ho Chi Minh Sarani

US Consulate

Shakespeare Sarani

Monapali

Gallerie 88

La Martiniere School

Race Course

Hospital Rd

Victoria Memorial & Museum

Cathedral Rd

Planetarium

Prerto Rd

Camac St

Loudon St

Entrance to Racecourse

Kidderpore Docks (for Andamans Ferry)

Polo Ground

St Paul's Cathedral

Academy of Fine Arts

AJC Bose Rd

Bengal Home Industries

Central Plaza

Tivoli Court

Woodlands Nursing Home

KIDDERPORE

Munshiganj Rd

Diamond Harbour Rd

AJC Bose Rd

Foreigners' Registration Office

Rabindra Sadan

Elgin Rd

Belvedere Rd

Tolly's Nullah

Bhowanipur Rd

Hospital Rd

Harish Mukherji Rd

Netaji Bhaven

Heysham Rd

BHAWANIPUR

Zoo

National Library

Ashutosh Mukherjee Rd

Bhawanipur

Sarat Bose Rd

P Barua Sarani

Nepal Consulate

Calcutta Hospital

Horticultural Gardens

Raghat Rd

Paddopukur Rd

To Kali Temple

To Tolly Club, Rabindra Sarobar, Seagull Media & Bookshop, Help Tourism, South City Mall &

To Birla Academy of Art & Culture &

To IIM, Behala & State Archaeological Museum

**Where to stay**
66/2B The
  Guest House **7**
Bodhi Tree & Art Café **1**
Park Palace **6**
Residency
  Guest House **8**
Sharani Lodge **9**
Taj Bengal &
  Chinoiserie
  Restaurant **3**
Vedic Village **5**

**Restaurants** 🍴
6 Ballygunge Place **12**
Anand **1**
Banana Leaf **2**
Bhojohori Manna **4**
Dolly's the Tea Shop **8**
Indian Coffee House **3**
Krystal Chopsticks **6**
Mainland China **5**
Mirch Masala **9**
Rehmania & Shiraz **7**

**Bars & clubs** 🍸
Floatel **10**
Tripti's **11**

glimpse into Bar Rooms crammed floor-to-ceiling with books, and bustling with black-robed lawyers (no cameras allowed).

**State Bank Archives and Museum** ⓘ *11th Fl, SBI, 1 Strand Rd, open Tue-Fri 1430-1700, free.* In a recent building designed to look period is a grand marble-floored repository of information; it also contains paintings of Raj India, furniture and memorabilia related to the early days of banking. The nearby **Floatel** bar (see page 54), on the Hooghly, is a good place to relax after wanderings.

**Esplanade** **Esplanade Mansions** is a stunning Art Nouveau building on Esplanade Row East, built in 1910 by Jewish millionaire David Ezra. At the other end of the street, the minarets and domes of **Tipu Sultan's Mosque**, built by Tipu's son in 1842, poke above market stalls selling stationery and little kebab restaurants. The **Ochterlony Monument** (1828), renamed Shahid Minar (Martyrs' Memorial) in 1969, was built as a memorial to Sir David Ochterlony, who led East India Company troops against the Nepalese in 1814-1816. The 46-m-tall Greek Doric column has an Egyptian base and is topped by a Turkish cupola.

**Eden Gardens** ⓘ *Daily 1200-1700.* Situated in the northwest corner of the Maidan (see below), the gardens were laid out in 1834 and named after Lord Auckland's sisters Emily and Fanny Eden. There are pleasant walks, a lake and a small Burmese pagoda (typical of this type of Pyatthat). Also here is the **Ranji Stadium** ⓘ *usually open for matches only, a small tip at Gate 14 gains entry on other days,* where the first cricket match was played in 1864. Revamped in 2011 for the Cricket World Cup, it attracts massive crowds for IPL and Test matches.

## The Maidan and around

Two hundred years ago this area was covered in dense jungle. Often called the 'lungs of the city', it is a unique green space, covering over 400 ha along Chowringhee (JL Nehru Road). Larger than New York's Central Park, it is perhaps the largest urban park in the

# 2 Central Kolkata

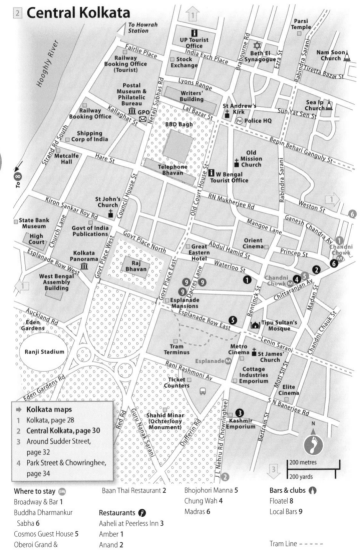

⮕ **Kolkata maps**

1 Kolkata, page 28
2 Central Kolkata, page 30
3 Around Sudder Street, page 32
4 Park Street & Chowringhee, page 34

**Where to stay** 🛏
Broadway & Bar 1
Buddha Dharmankur
Sabha 6
Cosmos Guest House 5
Oberoi Grand &

Baan Thai Restaurant 2

**Restaurants** 🍴
Aaheli at Peerless Inn 3
Amber 1
Anand 2

Bhojohori Manna 5
Chung Wah 4
Madras 6

**Bars & clubs** 🍸
Floatel 8
Local Bars 9

Tram Line - - - - -

world. In it stands Fort William and several clubhouses providing tennis, football, rugby, cricket and even crown green bowls. Thousands each day pursue a hundred different interests here: early morning yogis, model plane enthusiasts, weekend cricketers and performers earning their living, to vast political gatherings.

**Fort William** The massive Fort William was built by the British after their defeat in 1756, on the site of the village of Govindapur. Designed to be impregnable, it was roughly octagonal and large enough to house all the Europeans in the city in case of an attack. Water from the Hooghly was channelled to fill the wide moat and the surrounding jungle was cleared to give a clear field of fire; this later became the Maidan. The barracks, stables, arsenal, prison and St Peter's Church are still there, but the fort now forms the Eastern Region's Military Headquarters and entry is forbidden.

**Victoria Memorial** (1906-1921) ⓘ *T033-2223 1889-91, www.victoriamemorial-cal.org; gardens 0530-1815 (last entry 1745), Rs 10; museum Tue-Sun 1000-1700 (last entry 1630, very crowded on Sun), foreigners Rs 200, cameras not permitted inside; son et lumière show summer 1945, winter 1915, 45 mins, Rs 20 front seats, Rs 10 elsewhere.* Located in the far southeast corner of the Maidan, the white marble monument to Queen Victoria and the Raj was the brain-child of Lord Curzon. Designed in Italian Renaissance/Indo-Saracenic style, it stands in large, well-kept grounds with ornamental pools. A seated bronze Queen Victoria dominates the approach from the north, while a marble statue stands in the main hall where visitors sometimes leave flowers at her feet. The building is illuminated in the evening, when the musical fountain is a special draw. The statues over the entrance porches (including Motherhood, Prudence and Learning), and around the central dome (of Art, Architecture, Justice, Charity) came from Italy. The impressive weather vane, a 5-m-tall bronze winged Angel of Victory weighing three tonnes, looks tiny from below.

The principal gallery, covering the history of the city, is well presented and makes interesting reading. It includes some fascinating lithographs and illustrations of the city during the Raj period. The painting gallery has magnificent works by European artists in India from 1770-1835, including Zoffany, the two Daniells and Samuel Davis. Recently, the upper gallery of the Queen's Hall was reopened after more than a decade, and visitors can now walk around the inside of the rotunda again.

**St Paul's Cathedral** ⓘ *Cathedral Rd, 0900-1200, 1500-1800, 5 services on Sun.* East of the memorial, this is the original metropolitan church of British India. Completed in 1847, its Gothic tower (dedicated in 1938) was designed to replace the earlier steeples which were destroyed by earthquakes. The cathedral has a fine altar piece, three 'Gothic' stained-glass windows, two Florentine frescoes and the great West window by Burne-Jones. The original stained-glass East window, intended for St George's Windsor, was destroyed by a cyclone in 1964 and was replaced by the present one four years later.

**Academy of Fine Arts** ⓘ *2 Cathedral Rd, Tue-Sun 1500-2000 (ground floor galleries), 1200-1900 (museum), free.* The Academy was founded in 1933. The first floor museum has a newly restored gallery showing 33 pictures by Rabindranath Tagore, plus his writings and some personal effects. The textiles gallery and other sections have been closed for years, but

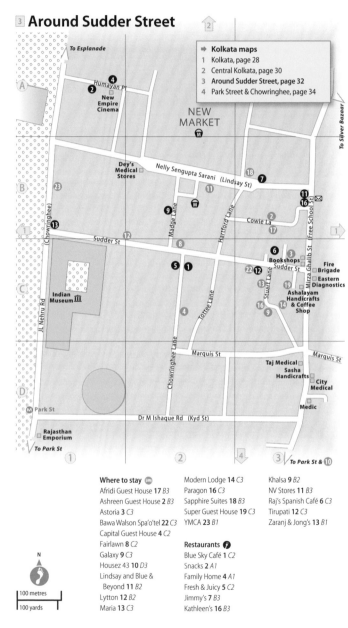

# 3 Around Sudder Street

**Kolkata maps**
1 Kolkata, page 28
2 Central Kolkata, page 30
3 Around Sudder Street, page 32
4 Park Street & Chowringhee, page 34

**Where to stay**
Afridi Guest House 17 *B3*
Ashreen Guest House 2 *B3*
Astoria 3 *C3*
Bawa Walson Spa'o'tel 22 *C3*
Capital Guest House 4 *C2*
Fairlawn 8 *C2*
Galaxy 9 *C3*
Housez 43 10 *D3*
Lindsay and Blue & Beyond 11 *B2*
Lytton 12 *B2*
Maria 13 *C3*
Modern Lodge 14 *C3*
Paragon 16 *C3*
Sapphire Suites 18 *B3*
Super Guest House 19 *C3*
YMCA 23 *B1*

Khalsa 9 *B2*
NV Stores 11 *B3*
Raj's Spanish Café 6 *C3*
Tirupati 12 *C3*
Zaranj & Jong's 13 *B1*

**Restaurants**
Blue Sky Café 1 *C2*
Snacks 2 *A1*
Family Home 4 *A1*
Fresh & Juicy 5 *C2*
Jimmy's 7 *B3*
Kathleen's 16 *B3*

may reopen soon. The ground floor galleries show changing exhibitions contemporary paintings and sculptures by Indian artists.

## Park Street and Chowringhee

Along Chowringhee, you can still see some of the old imposing structures with pillared verandas (designed by Italian architects as residences of prominent Englishmen), though modern high-rise buildings and a flyover have transformed the skyline of what was the ancient pilgrim route to Kalighat. Conveniently close to Chowringhee and Esplanade, **Sudder Street** is the focus for Kolkata's backpackers and attracts touts, beggars and the odd drug pusher.

> **Tip...**
> Beggars on Chowringhee and Park Street often belong to organized syndicates to whom they have to pay a large percentage of their earnings for the 'privilege' of working the area. Women asking for milk or rice for their baby are commonly deployed on Sudder Street.

**New Market** Just north of Sudder Street is the vast and archaic shopping hub of New Market, opened in 1874 as Sir Stuart Hogg Market, largely rebuilt following a fire in 1985 and recently revamped. The clock tower outside, which strikes every 15 minutes, was imported from England. It used to be said that you could buy anything from a needle to an elephant (on order) in one of its stalls. Today it's still worth a visit; arrive early in the morning to watch it come alive (many shops closed on Sundays).

**Indian Museum** ① *27 Chowringhee (JL Nehru Rd), T033-2286 1679, www.indian museumkolkata.org, Mar-Nov Tue-Sun 1000-1700, Dec-Feb 1000-1630, foreigners Rs 500; no bags allowed (there is a cloakroom).* Around the corner from Sudder Street is the Indian Museum possibly Asia's largest. The Jadu Ghar (House of Magic) was founded in 1814 and has an enormous collection. The colonnaded Italianate building around a central courtyard has 36 galleries (though sections are often closed for restoration). Parts are poorly lit and gathering dust so it is best to be selective. Highlights include: the stone statutory with outstanding exhibits from the Harappa and Mohenjo Daro periods; the Cultural Anthropology room with information on India's tribes; and the excellent new Mask Gallery (hidden on the fourth floor, up the stairs past the ground floor coin collection and library). There are some lovely miniature paintings, the Egyptian room has a popular mummy and the Plant Gallery is curiously beautiful, with jars, prints and samples filling every inch of space. The animals in the Natural History Gallery have been there since 1878, while the birds are so dirty they are all uniformly black in colour. The geological collection with Siwalik fossils is mind-bogglingly huge. Allow at least couple of hours.

**Asiatic Society** ① *1 Park St, T033-2229 0779, www.asiaticsocietycal.com. Mon-Fri 1000-1800, free. Bring a passport, and note that signing in is (at least) a triplicate process.* This is the oldest institution of Oriental studies in the world and was founded in 1784 by the great Orientalist, Sir William Jones. It is a treasure house of 150,000 books and 60,000 ancient manuscripts in most Asian languages, although permission is required to see specific pieces. The museum includes an Ashokan edict, rare coins and paintings. The library is worth a visit for its dusty travelogues and titles on the history of Kolkata. The original 1804 building is to the rear; you can ask to view the impressive staircase adorned with

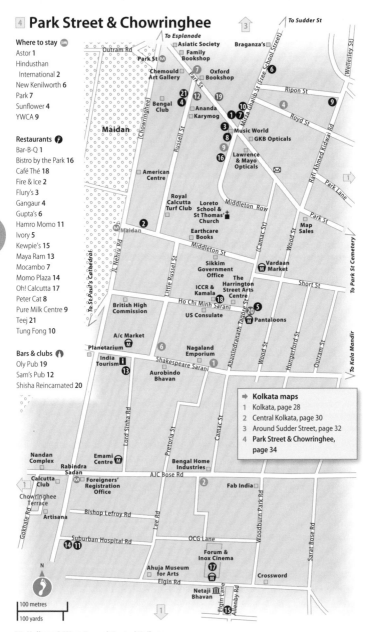

# 4 Park Street & Chowringhee

**Where to stay** 🛏
Astor 1
Hindusthan
  International 2
New Kenilworth 6
Park 7
Sunflower 4
YWCA 9

**Restaurants** 🍴
Bar-B-Q 1
Bistro by the Park 16
Café Thé 18
Fire & Ice 2
Flury's 3
Gangaur 4
Gupta's 6
Hamro Momo 11
Ivory 5
Kewpie's 15
Maya Ram 13
Mocambo 7
Momo Plaza 14
Oh! Calcutta 17
Peter Cat 8
Pure Milk Centre 9
Teej 21
Tung Fong 10

**Bars & clubs** 🎵
Oly Pub 19
Sam's Pub 12
Shisha Reincarnated 20

To Sudder St

To Esplanade
To Sudder St
Braganza's
Outram Rd
Park St
Asiatic Society
Family Bookshop
Chemould Art Gallery
Oxford Bookshop
Ripon St
Bengal Club
Ananda
Karymog
Music World
GKB Opticals
Lawrence & Mayo Opticals
Maidan
Royd St
American Centre
Royal Calcutta Turf Club
Loreto School & St Thomas' Church
Middleton Row
Earthcare Books
Middleton St
Park Lane
Park St
Map Sales
Sikkim Government Office
Vardaan Market
The Harrington Street Arts Centre
Short St
ICCR & Kamala
Ho Chi Minh Sarani
British High Commission
US Consulate
Pantaloons
A/c Market
Planetarium
India Tourism
Nagaland Emporium
Shakespeare Sarani
Aurobindo Bhavan
To St Paul's Cathedral
JL Nehru Rd
Maidan

**Kolkata maps**
1 Kolkata, page 28
2 Central Kolkata, page 30
3 Around Sudder Street, page 32
4 Park Street & Chowringhee, page 34

Nandan Complex
Emami Centre
Rabindra Sadan
Calcutta Club
Chowringhee Terrace
Foreigners' Registration Office
Bengal Home Industries
Fab India
Artisana
Bishop Lefroy Rd
AJC Bose Rd
Suburban Hospital Rd
OCG Lane
Forum & Inox Cinema
Ahuja Museum for Arts
Elgin Rd
Netaji Bhavan
Crossword

100 metres
100 yards

statues and paintings. Here also is the manuscript restoration department, where staff are pleased to explain the work they undertake.

**Park Street Cemetery** ⓘ *Daily 0800-1630, free, information booklet Rs 100, security guard opens gate and will expect you to sign the visitors' book.* The cemetery was opened in 1767 to accommodate the large number of British who died 'serving' their country. It is a peaceful paradise and a step into history, located on the south side of one of Kolkata's busiest streets, with a maze of soaring obelisks shaded by tropical trees. The heavily inscribed decaying headstones, rotundas, pyramids and urns have been restored, and gardeners are actively trying to beautify the grounds.

Several of the inscriptions make interesting reading. Death, often untimely, came from tropical diseases or other hazards such as battles, childbirth and even melancholia. More uncommonly, it was an excess of alcohol, or as for Sir Thomas D'Oyly, through "an inordinate use of the hokkah". Rose Aylmer died after eating too many pineapples! Tombs include those of Colonel Kyd, founder of the Botanical Gardens, the great oriental scholar Sir William Jones, and the fanciful mausoleum of the Irish Major-General 'Hindoo' Stuart.

**Scottish Cemetery** ⓘ *Karaya Rd, daily 0700-1730, free, pamphlet by donation to the caretaker.* Across AJC Bose Road is the smaller and far more derelict Scottish Cemetery, established in 1820. The Kolkata Scottish Heritage Trust began work in 2008 to restore some of the 1600 tumbledown graves but the undergrowth is rampant and jungle prevails. It is also known as the 'dissenters' graveyard', as this was where non-Anglicans were buried. Also nearby, on AJC Bose Road, is the enormous **Lower Circular Road Cemetery** created in 1840 when Park Street Cemetery became full.

## North Kolkata

potters, intellectuals and some interesting museums

### College Street
This is the heart of intellectual Kolkata with the **university** and several academic institutions, including the old **Sanskrit College** and the elite **Presidency College**. Europeans and Indian benefactors established the Hindu College (1817) to provide a liberal education. In 1855, this became the Presidency College. A centre for 19th-century Bengali writers, artists and reformers, it spawned the early 20th-century Swadeshi Movement. The famous **Indian Coffee House** (opened in 1944), cavernous haunt of the city's intelligentsia, has tonnes of atmosphere and is always packed despite the average coffee and food. Along the pavements are interesting second-hand book stalls.

**Ashutosh Museum of Indian Art** ⓘ *University Centenary Building, College Street, Mon-Fri 1100-1630, closed university holidays, Rs 10, camera Rs 200.* This is well maintained and worth a visit. The ground floor is packed with eastern Indian sculptures and terracotta tiles depicting figures. The first floor has colourful Bengali and Orissan folk art, faded textiles, and a hoard of paintings including 14th- to 19th-century miniatures, Kalighat paintings, Nepalese art and Tibetan *thankas*. Also look out for the model of the Senate Hall (1873-

## BACKGROUND

### Kolkata

Calcutta, as it came to be named, was founded by the remarkable English merchant trader Job Charnock in 1690. He was in charge of the East India Company factory (ie warehouse) in Hooghly, then the centre of British trade from eastern India. Attacks from the local Muslim ruler forced him to flee – first downriver to Sutanuti and then 1500 km south to Chennai. However, in 1690 he selected three villages – Kalikata, Sutanuti and Govindpur – where Armenian and Portuguese traders had already settled, leased them from Emperor Aurangzeb and returned to what became the capital of British India.

The first fort here, named after King William III (completed 1707), was on the site of the present BBD Bagh. A deep defensive moat was dug in 1742 to strengthen the fort – the Maratha ditch. The Maratha threat never materialized but the city was captured easily by the 20-year-old Siraj-ud-Daula, the new Nawab of Bengal, in 1756. The 146 British residents who failed to escape by the fort's river gate were imprisoned for a night in a small guard room about 6 m by 5 m with only one window – the infamous 'Black Hole of Calcutta'. Some records suggest 64 people were imprisoned and only 23 survived.

The following year Robert Clive re-took the city. The new Fort William was built, and in 1772 Calcutta became the capital of British administration in India, with Warren Hastings as the first Governor of Bengal. Some of Calcutta's most impressive colonial buildings were built in the years that followed when it became the first city of British India. It was also a time of Hindu and Muslim resurgence.

Colonial Calcutta grew as new traders, soldiers and administrators arrived, establishing their exclusive social and sports clubs. Trade in cloth, silk, lac, indigo, rice, areca nut and tobacco had originally attracted the Portuguese and British to Bengal. Later Calcutta's hinterland producing jute, iron ore, tea and coal led to large British firms setting up headquarters in the city. Calcutta prospered as the commercial and political capital of British India until 1911, when the capital was transferred to Delhi.

Calcutta had to absorb huge numbers of migrants immediately after Partition in 1947. And, when Pakistan ceased trading with India in 1949, Calcutta's economy suffered a massive blow: it lost its supplies of raw jute, and its failure to attract new investment created critical economic problems. In the late 1960s the Communist Party of India Marxist, the CPI(M), was elected; their dominance was to last over 30 years. From 2000 the CPI(M) was committed to a mixed economy and sought foreign private investment, and the city's economy experienced a much needed upturn. In the 2011 state assembly election the communist government was defeated after 34 years in power by the Trinamool Congress. Controversial politician Mamata Bannerjee, known as "Didi", remains the current Chief Minister and the first woman to hold this position. The city officially changed its name to Kolkata in 2001.

1960), which was pulled down to make way for the concrete monster of the present Centenary block in the days before heritage buildings were accorded any value.

## Howrah Bridge area

Howrah Bridge (Haora), or Rabindra Setu, was opened in 1943. This single-span cantilever bridge, a quintessential image of Kolkata, replaced the old pontoon (floating) bridge that first joined the city of Kolkata with Howrah and the railway station. To avoid affecting river currents

> **Tip...**
> At night Howrah bridge is illuminated, which makes a fine sight. If waiting for a night train at Howrah station, go to the first floor waiting rooms for a good view.

and silting, the two 80-m-high piers rise from road level; the 450-m span expands by a metre on a hot day. It is the busiest bridge in the world in terms of foot passengers (many with improbable loads on their heads). Wrestlers can be seen underneath and there is a daily **flower market** beneath the eastern end at Mullik Ghat, with piles of marigolds glowing against the mud. The pedestrian-free **Vidyasagar Setu Bridge**, further south, has eased the traffic burden slightly.

**Armenian Kolkata** Southeast of Howrah Bridge, the gorgeously well-kept **Armenian Church** of **Holy Nazareth** (1724) is a reminder of the important trading role the small Armenian community, who mostly came from Iran, played from the 17th century. The church is open 0600-1200 on weekdays or you can ask someone to open up in order to view the beautifully maintained interior. A gravestone in the compound is inscribed with the date 1630. The 150 or so Armenians in the city still hold a service in Armenian in one of their two churches in the city every Sunday. Their college on Mirza Ghalib Street (also the birthplace of William Makepeace Thackery in 1811) has boarding pupils from Armenia who are usually orphans. To the east of the Church of Holy Nazareth is the **Roman Catholic Cathedral** (1797), built by the Portuguese.

**Jewish Kolkata** The Jewish community, mostly Sephardic and of Baghdadi origin, was once very prominent in commerce in the city and numbered about 6000 before the Second World War. Their two synagogues are well maintained with stained-glass windows. The grander of the two is the church-like and cavernous **Moghan David Synagogue** (1884) ① *Canning St, daily 0900-1700*, while the nearby **Beth El Synagogue** ① *26/1 Pollock St, Sun-Fri 1000-1700*, is smaller. Just around the corner from the Moghan David Synagogue, on Brabourne Road hidden behind market stalls, is the older and derelict **Neveh Shalome Synagogue** (now inaccessible). To view the interior of the synagogues, it is necessary to get signed permission either from **Nahoum & Son's Bakery** ① *Shop F20, New Market, T033-6526 9936* (easiest), or from the office at 1 Hartford Lane. There are only around 30-40 elderly Jews left in the city, but they continue to congregate at Nahoum & Son's Bakery. The Jewish Girls School in Park Street no longer has Jewish pupils; in fact the vast majority of the girls are Muslims from a nearby neighbourhood.

**Chinese Kolkata** A few reminders that there was once a Chinatown in Kolkata remain in the form of Chinese 'churches'. Seek out the **Sea Ip Church** (1905), which has an intricately carved wooden altar and the **Nam Soon Church**, with a school at the rear. The latter is gorgeously maintained with bright paint, a huge bell and drum, and a little courtyard with trees. Both are willingly opened by the custodians. At the top of Bentinck Street, where it meets BB Ganguly Street, are several tiny old-fashioned shoe shops run by aging members of the Chinese community.

## Rabindra Sarani and around

Trams run along Rabindra Sarani, previously known as the Chitpur Road and one of the oldest streets in the city. Rising above the street-level are the three green domes, 27 minarets and multiple archways of **Nakhoda Mosque** (1926), Kolkata's principal mosque holding 10,000 worshippers.

**Rabindra Bharati Museum** ⓘ *6/4 Dwarakanath Tagore Lane (red walls visible down lane opposite 263 Rabindra Sarani), Mon-Fri 1000-1700, Sat 1000-1330, Sun and holidays 1100-1400, http://rbu.ac.in/museum/about_rb/.* A large brick gateway leads to the family home of Rabindranath Tagore, who won the Nobel Prize for Literature in 1913. It's a peaceful enclave away from the teeming chaos of Rabindra Sarani and showcases Tagore's life and works, as well as the 19th-century Renaissance movement in Bengal. Be sure to explore along all the corridors, as it's easy to miss the galleries of Indian and European art, and the Japanese exhibition rooms.

**Marble Palace** ⓘ *46 Muktaram Babu St, Tue, Wed, Fri-Sun 1000-1600. Free pass from WBTDC (see page 45) 24 hrs ahead, or baksheesh (Rs 20 per visitor) to the security man at the gate and a further tip to the attendant who will accompany you around. Shoes must be removed, no photography allowed.* Located in Chor Bagan ('Thieves' Garden'), the one-man collection of Raja Rajendra Mullick is housed in his ornate home (1835) with an Italianate courtyard, classical columns and Egyptian sphinxes. Family members still inhabit a portion of the house while servants' descendants live in the huts that encircle the grounds. Six sleeping marble lions and statuary grace the lawns and there is a veritable menagerie at the back of the garden. The galleries, disorganized and gathering dust, are crammed with statues, porcelain, clocks, mirrors, chandeliers and English (Reynolds), Dutch (Reubens) and Italian paintings. The pink, grey and white Italian marble floors are remarkable, as is the solid rosewood statue of Queen Victoria. Allow one hour to look round, or take a book and relax in the garden. The rambling two-floor museum has more than just curiosity appeal – it is one of Kolkata's gems.

## Northeast of the city centre

Northeast of the city centre, accessed from Belgachia Metro station, is a cluster of three Digambar Jain temples, one of the most tranquil spots in the city. The meticulously maintained and ornate **Paresnath Temple** ⓘ *0700-1200, 1500-2000, no leather*, is dedicated to the 10th Tirthankara. Consecrated around 1867, it is richly decorated with mirrors, Victorian tiles and Venetian glass mosaics.

**Clive's House** ⓘ *Off Jessore Rd in Nagarbajar, Dum Dum.* Difficult to find (and perhaps not worth the effort unless you are a true aficionado of Raj history) is the country home of the first governor general of the East India Company. It is the oldest colonial monument in Kolkata. For years, Bangladeshi immigrants lived in and around the derelict property until

## ON THE ROAD

## Worship of the clay goddess

Durga Puja, the 17th-century festival in honour of the clay goddess, precedes the full moon in late September/early October, when all offices and institutions close down and the metro only operates from the late afternoon.

Images of the 10-armed, three-eyed goddess, a form of Shakti or Kali astride her 'vehicle' the lion, portray Durga slaying Mahisasura, the evil buffalo demon. Durga, shown with her four children Lakshmi, Sarasvati, Ganesh and Kartik, is worshipped in thousands of brightly illuminated and beautifully decorated *pandals* (marquees). Traditionally these are made of bamboo and coloured cloth, but often modern *pandals* are veritable works of art constructed to complex designs and tapping into current themes or re-creating popular Indian landmarks. The priests perform prayers at appointed times in the morning and evening. On the fourth and last day of festivities, huge and often emotionally-charged processions follow devotees who carry the clay figures to be immersed in the river at many points along the banks. The potters return to collect clay from the river bank once again for the following year.

You can see the image makers in Kumartuli (see page 39) a few days earlier and visit the *pandals* early in the day, before they become intensely crowded. Local communities are immensely proud of their *pandals* and no effort is spared to put on the most impressive display. The images are decorated with intricate silver, golden or *shola* (white pith) ornaments; there are moving electric light displays, and huge structures are built (sometimes resembling a temple) in order to win competitions.

it was restored in 2008. The brick walls are being re-consumed by plant life and it requires some imagination to envisage its former glory.

### North along the Hooghly

Kumartuli Off Chitpur Road, the *kumars* or potters work all year, preparing clay images around cores of bamboo and straw. For generations they have been making life-size idols for the *pujas* or festivals, particularly of goddess Durga on a lion, slaying the demon. The images are usually unbaked since they are immersed in the holy river at the end of the festival. As the time of the *pujas* approaches, you will see thousands of images, often very brightly painted and gaudily dressed, awaiting the final finishing touch by the master painter. There are also *shola* artists who make decorations for festivals and weddings. The potters' area of Kumartuli is being slowly rebuilt, and concrete structures are replacing the towering bamboo workshops that were so very photogenic.

Belur Math ⓘ *Some 16 km north of the city, daily 0600-1200, 1600-1900.* Belur Math is the international headquarters of the **Ramakrishna Mission**, founded in 1899 by Swami Vivekananda, a disciple of the 19th-century Hindu saint Ramakrishna. He preached the unity of all religions,

Tip...
Ride the ferry boat (Rs 15) across the Hooghly between Belur Math and Dakshineshwar Temple for a lovely 20-minute journey at any time of day.

as symbolized in the architecture of the *Math* ('monastery'), which synthesizes Hindu, Christian and Islamic styles in a peaceful and meditative atmosphere.

**Dakshineshwar Kali Temple** ⓘ *0600-1200, 1500-1800, 1830-2100, no photography allowed inside. Buses from BBD Bagh go to Dunlop Intersection, from where it's a short auto ride to the temple; or trains run from Sealdah to Dakshineshwar.* On the opposite side of the river from Belur Math is the Dakshineshwar Temple, **a** huge Kali temple was built in 1847 by Rani Rashmoni. The 12 smaller temples in the courtyard are dedicated to Siva and there are also temples to Radha and Krishna. Because of the Rani's low caste, no priest would serve there until Ramakrishna's elder brother agreed and was succeeded by Ramakrishna himself. Here, Ramakrishna achieved his spiritual vision of the unity of all religions. The temple is crowded with colourfully clad devotees, particularly on Sundays when there are lengthy queues, and is open to all faiths.

## South Kolkata

temples, markets, gardens and museums

### Netaji Museum
*Netaji Bhavan, 38/1 Elgin Rd, www.netaji.org/museum, Tue-Sun 1100-1430 (last entry 1615), Rs 5, no photography.*

This museum remembers the mission of Subas Chandra Bose, the leader of the INA (Indian National Army), and is in the house where he lived before he had to flee the British oppressors. On the first floor, you can view his bedroom and study (where walls are painted with the tricolours of the Congress flag), although panes of glass prevent close inspection of his possessions. A detailed video is played in the second floor rooms showing old footage and giving a detailed explanation of his life's work. Interesting is the German Room, with a photo of Netaji meeting Hitler and information on Azad Hind and the Indo-German Friendship Society.

### Kalighat Kali Temple and around
*Off Ashok Mukherjee Rd, 0500-1500, 1700-2200.*

This is the temple to Kali (1809), the patron goddess of Kolkata, usually seen in her bloodthirsty form garlanded with skulls. There was an older temple here, where the goddess's little toe is said to have fallen when Siva carried her charred corpse in a frenzied dance of mourning, and she was cut into pieces by Vishnu's *chakra*. Where once human sacrifices were made (up until 1835, a boy was beheaded every Friday), the lives of goats are offered daily on two wooden blocks to the south of the temple.

When visiting the temple, priests will attempt to snare foreigners for the obligatory *puja*. A barrage may start as far away as 500 m from the temple. Don't be fooled in to handing over your shoes and succumbing to any priests until you are clearly inside the temple, despite being shown 'priest ID' cards. An acceptable minimum donation is Rs 50, books showing previous donations of Rs 3000 are doubtless faked. Having done the *puja*, you'll probably be left alone to soak up the atmosphere.

**Nirmal Hriday** Mother Teresa, an Albanian by birth, came to India to teach as a Loreto nun in 1931. She started her Order of the Missionaries of Charity in Kalighat to serve the destitute and dying 19 years later. Nirmal Hriday ('Pure Heart'), near the Kali Temple, the first home for the dying, was opened in 1952. Mother Teresa died on 5 September 1997 but her work continues. You may see nuns in their white cotton saris with blue borders busy working in the many homes, clinics and orphanages in the city.

## Gariahat

The neighbourhoods around Gariahat are more middle class and greener than Central Kolkata, but no less interesting, with plenty of good restaurants and small hotels.

**Birla Mandir** ⓘ *0600-1100 and 1630-2030.* On Gariahat Road, the shiny white edifice pulls in a lot of devotees and is particularly impressive when lit up at night. Taking 22 years to complete, another gift of the Birla family, it is modelled on the Lingaraj Temple at Bhubaneshwar and is covered with carvings both inside and out. No photos are permitted inside. Just north of the temple is the **CIMA Gallery** (see page 55) which is worth a look.

**Gariahat Market** South of the Birla Mandir, beyond the southeast corner of Gariahat Crossing, is Gariahat Market which specializes in fish and is a fascinating hive of activity, especially in the early morning. Take a walk west from the crossing along 2-km Rash Behari Avenue, one of the city's liveliest streets, lined with sari stalls, *menhdi* (henna) artists, momo vendors and vegetable sellers; it's especially atmospheric at dusk.

**Birla Academy of Art and Culture** ⓘ *108/109 Southern Av, T033-2466 2843, Tue-Sun 1600-2000.* A couple of blocks south in a modern high-rise, the Academy concentrates on medieval and contemporary paintings and sculpture. The ground floor sculpture gallery has been recently remodelled, and displays some beautiful pieces including Buddhist and Hindu statues. It is well lit and worth visiting. The upper levels host changing art exhibitions.

## Rabindra Sarobar

The large and pleasant lake of Rabindra Sarobar is shaded by ancient trees and surrounded by a pathway perfect for joggers and walkers. There are several rowing clubs (the oldest dates from 1858), and Laughing Clubs meet in the mornings (around 0600) to mix yoga and group laughing.

A road from the southwest corner of the lake leads to the trim little **Japanese Buddhist Temple** (1935), the oldest temple of the Nichiren sect in India. Visitors are welcomed, and can join in the hypnotic prayers by beating handheld drums (at dawn and dusk). A slim congregation of ex-Ghurkhas, Nepali ladies and bemused Bengalis are drawn in. The interior is restful with an elaborate golden shrine, gaudy flowers, ornamental lanterns and origami birds which somehow come together to pleasing effect.

> **Tip...**
> It's possible to walk from the Buddhist Temple, via Dhakuria Bridge, to the **Dakshinapan** shopping complex (see page 57) and refresh at **Dolly's The Tea Shop** (see page 53).

## Alipore

South of the Maidan, the elite address of Alipore is home to a couple of sights.

**National Library** ⓘ *Belvedere Rd.* The National Library was once the winter residence of the Lieutenant Governors of Bengal. Built in the Renaissance Italian style, with a double row of classical columns, it is approached through a triple arched gateway and a drive between mahogany and mango trees. The library itself, the largest in the country with over eight million books, is now mainly housed in an adjacent newer building; sadly, the old building can no longer be entered.

**Kolkata Zoo** ⓘ *Opposite the library. Fri-Wed 0900-1700, Rs 10.* Opened in 1876, the zoo houses a wide variety of animal and bird life. The white tigers from Rewa and the tigon – a cross between a tiger and a lion – are the rarest animals. A reptile house and aquarium are across the road. There are restaurants and picnics are permitted, but it's often terrifyingly busy (particularly at the weekend).

**Agri-Horticultural Gardens** ⓘ *Alipore Rd, 0600-1300 and 1400-1830, Rs 10.* The expansive gardens are the most peaceful green space in the city. The Horticultural Society was started in 1820 by the Baptist missionary William Carey. Bring a book; you'll be the only visitor during the week.

### State Archaeological Museum

*Next to Behala tram depot, 1 Satyen Roy Rd, off Diamond Harbour Rd, Behala, Wed-Sun 1000-1630 (last entry 1600), Rs 5. Shared autos run from Kalighat metro to Behala, finishing close to the museum entrance.*

This little-visited yet well-presented museum has seven galleries over two floors, housed in a modern structure adjacent to the original colonial building. Galleries are devoted to West Bengal sites, such as the Buddhist remains of Nandadirghi Vihara near Malda, and the terracotta Hindu temples in Purulia. There's a meagre selection of local stone sculpture, intricate metal work, and a selection of Bengali paintings including Kalighat Pat (mostly religious in nature, but the famous *Two Women and a Rose* is a notable secular exception), and Murshidabad-style painting.

### Botanical Gardens

*20 km south from BBD Bagh, 0700-1700, Rs 50, avoid Sun and public holidays when it is very crowded, catch a bus from Esplanade; minibuses and CTC buses (No C-12) ply the route.*

Kolkata's Botanical Gardens, on the west bank of the Hooghly, were founded in 1787 by the East India Company. The flourishing 250-year-old banyan tree, with a circumference of almost 400 m, is perhaps the largest in the world. The original trunk was destroyed by lightning in 1919 but over 2800 offshoots form an impressive sight. The avenues of Royal Cuban palms and mahogany trees are impressive and there are interesting and exotic specimens in the herbarium and collections of ferns and cactii. The gardens are peaceful and deserted during the week and make a welcome change from the city.

There are several interesting places for a day's outing north of Kolkata in Hooghly District. When the Mughals lost power, several of the ancient seats of earlier rulers of Bengal became centres of foreign trade. Many European nations had outposts along the river. The Portuguese and British settled at Hooghly; the Dutch chose Chinsura; the French, Chandernagore; the Danes, Serampore; the Greeks had an outpost at Rishra, and the Germans and Austrians had one at Bhadreswar.

These old colonial towns straggle up the west bank of the Hooghly, providing insight into contemporary small-town life in Bengal as well as preserving some beautiful old colonial and Muslim buildings. It's best to take a train (buses are slow); avoid peak hours, and keep an eye on your possessions.

## Barrackpur

In Barrackpur, on the eastern side of the Hooghly (25 km north of Kolkata), the riverside **Gandhi Ghat** is a picturesque spot. There is **Gandhi Memorial Museum** and a pleasant garden in memory of Jawaharlal Nehru. The bronze Raj statues, removed from their pedestals in Central Kolkata after Independence, have found their way to the gardens of the bungalow of the former governor (Flagstaff House). The tower was part of the river signalling system. The town is accessed by train from Sealdah station.

## Shrirampur (Serampore)

Founded by the Danes in 1616 as Fredricnagore, Serampore, became a Danish colony in 1755. From the early 19th century it was the centre of missionary activity, until sold to the East India Company in 1845. The Government House, two churches (one of which is closed and unsafe to enter), the Old Court House (which is being renovated) and a Danish cemetery remain. There is a **College of Textile Technology** ⓘ *12 Carey Rd, 1000-1630 (Sat 1000-1300)*. The Baptist missionaries Carey, Marshman and Ward came to Serampore since they were not welcomed by the English administrators in Calcutta. They set up the Baptist Mission Press, which by 1805 was printing in seven Indian languages. **Serampore College** (1818) ⓘ *T033-2662 2322, Mon-Fri 1000-1600, Sat 1000-1300, with permission from the principal*, India's first Christian theological college and still operating as such, was allowed to award degrees by the Danish king in 1829. The library has rare Sanskrit, Pali and Tibetan manuscripts and the Bible in more than 40 Asian languages. Serampore is half an hour on a local train from Howrah station.

## Chandernagore

The former French colony, which dates back to 1673, was one of the tiny pockets of non-British India that did not gain Independence in 1947, but was handed over to India after a referendum in 1950. The churches, convents and cemeteries of the French are still there, although the old French street names have been replaced by Bengali ones. The former **Quai de Dupleix**, with its riverfront benches, still has a somewhat Gallic air. The Bhubanesvari and Nandadulal temples are worth visiting, especially during **Jagaddhatri Puja**. The **Institute Chandernagore** ⓘ *at the Residency, Mon-Sat except Thu 1600-1830, Sun 1100-1700*, has interesting documents and relics of the French in India. The orange-painted Italian missionary church (1726) also stands witness to Chandernagore's European past.

## Chinsura

The Dutch acquired Chinsura from the Nawab of Murshidabad in 1628 and built the **Fort Gustavus**, but it was exchanged with Sumatra (Indonesia) and became British in 1825. The octagonal Dutch church (1678) with its cemetery nearby, a 17th-century Armenian church and three East India Company barracks remain. The Dutch are still remembered at the **Shandesvar Siva Temple** on special occasions, when the lingam is bizarrely decked in Western clothes and a Dutch sword!

## Hooghly

The Portuguese set up a factory in Hooghly in 1537 but Emperor Shah Jahan took the important trading post in 1632. The East India Company built their factory in 1651, destroyed in skirmishes marking the following six years, but Clive regained Hooghly for the company in 1757. The **Shi'a Imambara of Hazi Mohammed Mohasin** (1836-1876) has fine marble inlay decoration, a silver pulpit and elaborate lanterns. In **Chota Pandua**, nearby, interesting Muslim buildings include the ruins of the 14th-century Bari Masjid which has elements of Buddhist sculpture. In Rajbalhat, the **Amulya Pratnasala Museum** ⓘ *Thu-Tue 1400-2100, closed 2nd and 4th Tue of the month*, exhibits sculpture, coins, terracottas and manuscripts.

## Bandel

Bandel (Portuguese *bandar* or wharf) is now a railway junction town. The Portuguese built **Bandel Church** to Our Lady of the Rosary around 1660, on the site of an older Augustinian monastery. The keystone of the original church (1599), perhaps the earliest in Bengal, is on the riverside gate. Destroyed in 1640 by Shah Jahan, the church was reinstated 20 years later. The seafaring Portuguese believed that the statue of Our Lady of Happy Voyages in the bell tower could work miracles. Lost in the river, while being carried to save it from Shah Jahan's soldiers, it miraculously reappeared two centuries later. The 18th-century stone and terracotta **Hanseswari Temple** is 4 km away.

## Tribeni and Pandua (Hooghly District)

Originally *Saptagram* (seven villages), **Tribeni** (three rivers) is particularly holy, being at the confluence of the Ganga, Saraswati and Kunti. It has many Hindu temples and 11th- to 12th-century Vaishnavite and Buddhist structures. The remains of the **Mazar of Zafarkhan Ghazi** (1313), the earliest mausoleum in eastern India, shows how black basalt sculpture and columns of earlier Hindu temples and palaces were incorporated into Muslim buildings. To the west, **Pandua** (not to be confused with the site further north; see page 74) has several remains of the Pala and Sena periods. Shah Sufi-ud-din is thought to have built the 39-m **Victory Tower** after defeating the local Hindu ruler in 1340. Its circular base had a court house. Outside, a staircase spirals up the fluted surface, while inside there is enamelled decoration. Hoards of Kushana and Gupta Dynasty gold coins have been found in nearby **Mahanad**.

## Kalna

The town north of Pandua, centred on the **Maharaja of Burdwan's Palace**, has several fine 18th-century terracotta temples. Look for the *Ramayana* scenes on the large Lalji (1739), Krishna panels on the Krishnachandra (1752), assorted friezes on the Ananta Vasudeva (1754) and the later Pratapesvara (1849). Across the way is the unusual circular **Siva Temple** (1809) with 108 small double-vaulted shrines. Kalna has trains from Kolkata, and there are rickshaws at the station, 3 km from the temples.

## ON THE ROAD

### Recommended reading for Kolkata

*A Dead Hand: A Crime in Calcutta* by Paul Theroux – a murder-mystery that will interest volunteers and cynics alike.
*Begums, Thugs and White Mughals* by Fanny Parkes – Calcutta features in the lively journals of an intrepid female traveller during the time of the East India Company.
*Bengal Nights* by Mircea Eliade – a semiautobiographical love story first published in Romanian in 1933 and only published in English 60 years later, after the death of one of the main protagonists.
*City of Joy* by Dominique Lapierre – an essential Kolkata read.
*The Lives of Others* by Neel Mukherjee allows insight into the minds and lives of a Calcutta family in the 1960s, and highlights the Marxist history of the state.
*Walking Calcutta* by Keith Humphreys – maps and fascinating information that open up the city's backstreets and secret corners.

### Nabadwip

The birthplace of Sri Chaitanya – the 14th-century Bengali religious reformer – is a pilgrimage centre for his followers, and the river ghats are lined with temples where devotees worship by singing *keertans* and *bhajans*. **International Society for Krishna Consciousness (ISKCON)** has a **Chandrodaya Mandir** ⓘ *Mayapu, across the river, until 1300*, and a guesthouse (inexpensive dorms, air-conditioned rooms and cheap meals). Nabadwip has trains from Sealdah and Howrah, and ferries across to Mayapur.

### Listings Kolkata *maps p28, p30, p32 and p34*

### Tourist information

**British Council**
*L&T Chambers, 16 Camac St, www. britishcouncil.org/indea.htm. Mon-Sat 1100-1900.*
Good for UK newspapers, reference books.

**India Tourism**
*4 Shakespeare Sarani, T033-2282 5813. Mon-Fri 0930-1800, Sat 0900-1300.*
Can provide a city map and also information for all India.

**West Bengal Tourism Development Corporation (WBTDC)**
*BBD Bagh, T033-2248 8271, www.wbtourism. gov.in. Mon-Fri 1030-1630, Sat 1030-1300; also a counter at the station in Howrah.*
More useful.

### Where to stay

Watch out for the 10% luxury tax and 10% service charge in the higher price brackets. Medium-price and budget hotels attracting foreigners are concentrated in the Sudder St area.

#### Central Kolkata

**$ Broadway**
*27A Ganesh Chandra Av, T033-2236 3930, www.broadwayhotel.in.*
Amazingly good-value hotel in a characterful building that hasn't changed much since it opened in 1937. Very clean rooms are non-a/c but airy with powerful fans, antique furniture and Bengali-red floors, towels, some with common bath, plus 24-hr checkout. Noisy on

the lower levels at the front. The bar is very appealing (see Bars and clubs, page 54).

### $ Buddha Dharmankur Sabha
*1 Buddhist Temple St, Bow Bazar, T033-2211 7138, www.bengalbuddhist.com.*
Run by the Bengal Buddhist Association and with plenty of monks wandering around, cheap clean rooms with twin beds, fans, decent shared bathrooms. A/c options with bath attached are a bit larger, with a few sticks of furniture. The compound gates are locked at 2230; call ahead to reserve.

### $ Cosmos Guest House
*Ground floor, 9 Chittaranjan Av, T033-2236 1383.*
Decent simple rooms aren't huge but have fresh paint, clean bedding, TV and good bathrooms. At the rear of the building, so surprisingly quiet. A good cheap choice for single travellers, also a/c rooms. There are 2 other hotels in the same building should Cosmos be full (which they often are).

## Park Street, Chowringhee and Sudder Street
Kyd St has changed its name to Dr Md Ishaque Rd and Free School St is also called Mirza Ghalib St.

### $$$$ Oberoi Grand
*15 Chowringhee (JL Nehru), T033-2249 2323, www.oberoihotels.com.*
Atmospheric Victorian building opposite the Maidan, exquisitely restored, suites with giant 4-posters, all rooms are spacious, those with balconies overlook the garden and pool are charming, bathrooms a tad old-fashioned but in keeping with the colonial style, excellent Thai restaurant and 24-hr **Le Terrasse** with international cuisine, billiards in the bar, lovely pool for guests, wonderful spa. Reasonable prices available online for a standard room.

### $$$$ Park
*17 Park St, T033-2249 9000, www.theparkhotels.com.*
Trendy designer hotel, one of Kolkata's most reputable, good restaurants, nightclubs, health club, 24-hr café, service can be disappointing, entrance themed on underground car park. Go online for the best discounts.

### $$$$-$$$ Astor
*15 Shakespeare Sarani, T033-2282 9957-9, www.astorkolkata.com.*
In a red-brick colonial building, comfortable a/c rooms with bath tubs, inferior annexe, have not retained original features, although public areas have fared better. The tiny blue-lit bar is decent, and **Plush** lounge-bar is fun. Breakfast included, mini-bar, off-season discounts, free Wi-Fi.

### $$$ Lindsay
*8-A Lindsay St, T033-3021 8666, http://thelindsay.in.*
Refurbished hotel towering over New Market, mainly for business travellers, good breakfast, gym. Smart **Blue & Beyond** rooftop restaurant/bar has panoramic city views and great food.

### $$$ Lytton
*14 Sudder St, T033-2249 1875-9, www.lyttonhotelindia.com.*
Comfortable, tastefully furnished rooms with flatscreen TVs, a/c bar, efficient and attracts a business clientele, breakfast included.

### $$$ New Kenilworth
*1 & 2 Little Russell St, T033-2282 3939, www.kenilworthhotels.com.*
A very comfortable and attractive hotel, though overpriced at rack rates (excellent deals online). Foyer is all marble and chandeliers, but modern rooms are neutrally furnished with soft lighting, minibar, and nice bathrooms. The older period building contains suites and the appealing **Big Ben**

English-style pub, with a pool table and sports TV, plus there's a spa.

### $$$ Sapphire Suites
*15 Lindsay St, T033-2252 3052-4,*
*www.sapphiresuites.in.*
29 a/c rooms in a new hotel in an attractive period building, right next to New Market. Rooms have sleek black and white furnishings, flatscreen TVs, bathrobes, tea/coffee facilities. Breakfast included, good multicuisine restaurant and fitness centre. Deals online.

### $$$-$$ Bawa Walson Spa'o'tel
*5A Sudder St, T033-2252 1512,*
*http://m-walson.bawahotels.com.*
An unlikely situation for a Spa'o'tel, but the **Walson** is immaculate with Thai accents throughout. Rooms are wood and white, swish shower rooms, free Wi-Fi, open-air Arabic restaurant. Big discounts possible.

### $$$-$$ Housez 43
*43 Mirza Ghalib St, T033-2227 6020,*
*https://thesparkhotels.com.*
A 'value boutique' hotel with contemporary, well-presented rooms, nice public areas with leather beanbags and seats, restaurant, elevator, breakfast included in the colourful café, pleasant staff.

### $$ Astoria Hotel
*6 Sudder St, near fire station, T033-2252 2241,*
*www.astoria.in.*
Offers 41 rooms of a good standard, after being recently renovated. All have a/c, hot water, and free Wi-Fi, it's a good standard for the price. Great top-floor room with a terrace.

### $$ Fairlawn
*13A Sudder St, T033-2252 1510/8766,*
*www.fairlawnhotel.com.*
A Calcutta institution, the old-fashioned but characterful rooms have a/c, TV, hot water, and are comfortable. Semi-formal meals at set times aren't the best, but breakfast and afternoon tea are included. The hotel

provides a throwback to the Raj, bric-a-brac everywhere, photos cover all the communal spaces, quite a place and the garden terrace is great for a beer.

### $ Afridi Guest House
*Opposite Ashreen Guest House (see below),*
*calcutta_guest house@yahoo.com.*
Most rooms share bathrooms, some have a/c, most have TV, but many rooms are windowless. Sheets are clean and standards better than many Sudder St options. Try and book ahead, though that's easier said than done.

### $ Ashreen Guest House
*2 Cowie Lane, T033-2252 0889,*
*ashreen_guesthouse@yahoo.com.*
Modern rooms with above-average facilities (for Sudder St) with TV and hot water, a suitable place to break yourself into Kolkata gently, however prices are ever escalating while standards slip. Pick-up for late night flights.

### $ Capital Guest House
*11B Chowringhee Lane, T033-2252 0598.*
Tucked away from the road in a freshly painted old building, Capital is relatively quiet and all rooms have TV and private bath, though ones with windows are more expensive. Good value compared to nearby options but not a place to meet other travellers.

### $ Galaxy
*3 Stuart Lane, T033-2252 4565,*
*hotelgalaxy@vsnl.net.*
12 good tiled rooms with attached bath and TV, some with a/c, a decent choice but often full with long-stayers. Try at around 1030 just after checkout.

### $ Maria
*5/1 Sudder St, T033-2252 0860.*
24 clean, basic rooms (hard beds), some with bath, dorm, internet, TV in the 'lobby', hot

water, water filter for guests' use. Popular budget place with a good atmosphere.

### $ Modern Lodge
*1 Stuart Lane, T033-2252 4960.*
Very popular, 14 rooms, attached or shared bath, cheapest at ground level, prices rise as you go up to the breezy rooftop, pleasant lobby with plants but sinister 'lounge', quirky staff, no reservations so try at 1000.

### $ Paragon
*2 Stuart Lane, T033-2252 2445.*
Textbook backpacker haunt with 45 rooms, some tiny and prison-like but it's clean just about (some doubles have attached bath) and mixed sex dorms (with shared/private bath), rooftop rooms are better. Water heater to fill buckets. Open communal spaces, indifferent management.

### $ Sunflower Guest House
*7 Royd St, T033-2229 9401,*
*www.sunflowerguesthouse.com.*
An airy 1950s building with very clean well-maintained rooms, TV, hot water, more costly with a/c and newer bathrooms. Spacious lounge area, the numerous staff are kindly. Good location, near Sudder St but out of the backpacker scene. No single room rates.

### $ Super Guest House
*30A Mirza Ghalib St, T033-2252 0995,*
*super_guesthouse@hotmail.com.*
This guesthouse has some of the cleanest rooms in the area for the price, all a/c with hot bath, tiled and simple box rooms. Be sure to ask for a room that does not suffer noise from the daily live music in **Super Pub Bar**. No single rates.

### $ YMCA
*25 Jl Nehru Rd, T033-2249 2192.*
17 rooms, some a/c, all with bath, geyser and TV, in large, rambling colonial building, clean linen, recently renovated but check room first as some are nicer than others. Helpful staff, rates include bed tea and breakfast. The oldest YMCA in Asia.

### $ YWCA
*1 Middleton Row, T033-2265 2494,*
*www.ywcacalcutta.org.*
Old colonial building with good atmosphere, airy verandas and tennis courts. Some rooms with bath, but doubles with shared bath have windows, dorm, all spotless, very friendly staff. Rates include breakfast, alcohol forbidden, a pleasant if shabby oasis in the city. A recommended alternative to Sudder St, especially for female travellers.

---

### South Kolkata
South Kolkata is a more salubrious area, where quiet residential streets hide some good (mainly mid-range) guesthouses. Excellent little restaurants and vibrant markets are in plentiful supply.

### $$$$ Hindusthan International
*235/1 AJC Bose Rd, T033-2283 0505,*
*www.hhihotels.com.*
Comfortable quiet rooms on 8 floors are priced right, but staff are distracting with their demands for tips. The food is nothing special although there are a couple of quite cool bars/coffee shop and **Underground** nightclub is popular, pool and spa. Big discounts possible.

### $$$$ Taj Bengal
*34B Belvedere Rd, Alipore, T033-2223 3939,*
*www.tajhotels.com.*
Opulent and characterful, several restaurants are plush, imaginative, intimate, with good food, leisurely service, unusual Bengali breakfast, **Khazana** shop is excellent.

### $$ 66/2B The Guest House
*66/2B Purna Das Rd, T033-2464 6422/1,*
*www.662btheguesthouse.com.*
On a tree-lined street with some great restaurants a 2-min walk away, this cheerful place is well furnished, with decent baths,

all rooms have a/c, geysers and flatscreens. A more relaxing area to stay in. Breakfast included, as is Wi-Fi. Recently refurbished.

### $$ The Bodhi Tree
*48/44 Swiss Park (near Rabindra Sarovar metro), T033-2424 6534, www.bodhitreekolkata.com.*
Simply beautiful little boutique hotel with just 6 rooms, each uniquely furnished in a different regional style (eg rural Bengal, with mud-plastered walls), and a $$$ penthouse. The in-house art-café is a delight (see Coffee shops, page 53), dinner is available, business centre, free Wi-Fi, small library, serves alcohol. Prices are very reasonable for a special experience.

### $$ Park Palace
*Singhi Villa, 49/2 Gariahat Rd, T033-2461 9108-11, www.parkpalacehotel.co.in.*
The main draws are the peaceful residential area, **Mirch Masala** restaurant/bar next door, and the roof terrace with excellent views. Rooms have fitted furniture and are large yet cosy, if twee. Ask for the 20% discount. Staff delightful. Behind **Pantaloons**, just off Gariahat Rd.

### $$ The Residency Guest House
*50/1C Purna Das Rd, T033-2466 9382, www.theresidency.co.in.*
A very appealing mid-range hotel, with clean tiled rooms, quality furnishings, a/c, TV, good bathrooms and comfortable beds. Close to Gariahat markets, but on a quiet street.

### $$ Tollygunge Club
*120 Deshapran Sasmal Rd, T033-2473 4539, www.tollygungeclub.org.*
On the south side of the city in 100 acres of grounds with an 18-hole golf course, swimming pool, tennis and other activities. Good bar and restaurants, one of which is open air. The place has charm and atmosphere which helps you overlook worn-out towels and casual service. Ask

for a renovated room, and enjoy the colonial feel. An interesting mid-range choice.

### $ Sharani Lodge
*71/K Hindustan Park, T033-2463 5717, gautam_sharani@rediffmail.com.*
In a quiet street, yet very close to hectic Rash Behari Av, this well-maintained and well-run lodge has an old-fashioned Indian ambiance. The a/c rooms are not worth really worth the extra money, but non-a/c are a great deal, those with common bath also share balconies at the front, all have TV, towels and plenty of space. There's a second building, across Rash Behari, with lovely little outdoor terrace (again, non-a/c rooms are more spacious and attractive than a/c ones).

## Other areas

### $$$$ Vedic Village
*T(0)9830025900, www.thevedicvillage.com.*
In Rajarhat, 20 mins from the airport on the eastern edge of the city, but a world away from the rest of Kolkata. The appeal is the clean air and rural surrounds as much as the luxurious rooms, fabulous pool and of course the spa. Top-end villas and suites are stunning while studio rooms are not unreasonably priced when compared to other options in the city.

## Restaurants

Licensed restaurants serve alcohol (some are unpleasant places to eat in since the emphasis is on drink). Be prepared for a large surcharge for live (or even recorded) music. This, plus taxes, can double the price on the menu.

## Central Kolkata

### $$$ Aaheli and Oceanic
*At the Peerless Inn, 12 JL Nehru Rd, www.peerlesshotels.com/Kolkata.*

**Aaheli** has an excellent menu of Bengali specialities, carefully selected from around the state by the chef, open from 1900. **Oceanic** has interesting seafood and is more pricey, open lunch and dinner. Both are comfortable with a/c and serve alcohol.

### $$$-$$ Amber
*11 Waterloo St. Open 1100-2330.*
2 floors of North Indian and continental delights (best for meat tandoori), generous helpings, fast service. **Essence** on 2nd floor fancies itself as a cocktail bar, but alcohol is served in both. Functional bar on the ground floor is strictly no women. Also has a smaller restaurant on Middleton Row, open 1200-1600 and 1900-2300.

### $$-$ Anand
*19 Chittaranjan Ave. Open 0900-2130, Sun from 0700, closed Wed.*
Great South Indian food. Mammoth *dosas*, stuffed *iddli*, all-vegetarian, family atmosphere and warmly decorated. Barefoot waiters are efficient. Big queues at weekends.

### $$-$ Bhojohori Manna
*Esplanade. Open 1130-2130 (closed for cleaning 1630-1800).*
Branch of the Bengali chain, with budget prices for veg dishes and pricier fish items. Ticks on the whiteboard indicate availability, choice can be limited in the evenings as they sell out.

### $$-$ Chung Wah
*13A Chittaranjan Av. Open 1100-2300.*
This hectic restaurant is functional and basic, with curtained-off booths along the sides. Hugely popular and with a large menu, it attracts a mostly male clientele, alcohol served. Recommended for the old-style atmosphere rather than the spicy Chinese food. Lone women are not encouraged.

### $ Madras Restaurant
*25/B Chittaranjan Av.*
A simpler setting than nearby **Anand** and slightly cheaper, but still has a/c. The list of *dosa* and *uttampams* is endless, plus there are a few Chinese dishes. Go between 1130-1530 for the South Indian *thalis*.

## Coffee shops, sweets and snacks

Indian Coffee House
*Albert Hall, just off College St.*
A must for its history and atmosphere (see page 35).

## Park Street, Chowringhee and Sudder Street
Visitors craving Western fast food will find plenty of familiar names around Park St.

### $$$ Baan Thai
*Oberoi Grand (see Where to stay, page 46).*
Excellent selection, imaginative decor, Thai-style seating on floor, or chairs and tables.

### $$$ Bar-B-Q
*43 Park St, T033-2229 9916.*
Always popular, always delicious. 3 sections serving Indian and Chinese food, bar.

### $$$ Bistro by the Park
*2A Middleton Row.*
It's near the park rather than 'by' it, but this attractive contemporary place serves world cuisine (including Southeast Asian, Middle Eastern) with the main focus on Italian fare (salads, pockets, pizzas, etc). Serves alcohol.

### $$$ Ivory
*Block D, 5th floor, 22 Camac St, www.ivory kitchen.com. Daily 1230-1500, 1900-2230.*
Slightly formal and functional, yet pleasingly decorated in ivory tones, dishes encompass a wide selection of Oriental and international dishes, with an Indian twist. Top-class dining.

### $$$ Zaranj and Jong's
*26 JL Nehru Rd.*
Adjacent restaurants, both stylish, subdued decor, excellent food. Try *pudina paratha*, *murgh makhani*, tandoori fish in **Zaranj**, or delectable Burmese fare in **Jong's**.

### $$ Fire and Ice
*Kanak Building, Middleton St, www. fireandicepizzeria.com. Open 1100-2330.*
Pizzas here are the real deal, service is excellent, and the ambience relaxing. Decor is very much what you would expect from a pizza place at home.

### $$ Flury's
*18 Park St.*
Classic Kolkata venue with hit-and-miss Western menu, but pastries and afternoon tea are winners and the bakery has brown bread. It's an institution.

### $$ Gangaur
*2 Russell St.*
A wide menu of Indian delights, if you can resist the superb *thali* (1130-1530). Afterwards head next door for Bengali sweets.

### $$ Jimmy's
*14D Lindsay St.*
Chinese. Small, a/c, good *momos*, Szechuan dishes, ice cream. Alcohol served.

### $$ Mocambo
*25B Park St.*
International. A/c, pleasant lighting, highly descriptive menu. Long-standing reliable favourite.

### $$ Peter Cat
*18A Park St (entrance on Middleton Row).*
Chiefly Indian, with some international dishes. Good kebabs and sizzlers, hilarious menu of cheap cocktails, pleasant ambience but can rush you on busy weekend nights. No booking system, expect to queue outside.

### $$ Teej
*2 Russell St.*
Pure vegetarian Rajasthani delights washed down with cold beer, in a colourful *haveli-*esque setting.

### $$ Tung Fong
*Mirzah Ghalib St.*
Quality Chinese food for a reasonable price, the setting spacious and subtly Asian, white linens and Ming vases. Great Manchurian dishes, good fish and chilli garlic paneer, excellent desserts. Super-swift service.

### $$-$ Gupta's
*53C Mirza Ghalib St. Open 1100-2300.*
Excellent Indian and Chinese. More intimate and softly lit upstairs, low ceilings (beware of the fans), try fish *tikka peshwari* and *bekti tikka*, alcohol reasonably priced.

### $ Blue Sky Café
*3 Sudder St.*
Chiefly Western. Very popular travellers' meeting place, a/c, always full and cramped, opinions on food vary, however.

### $ Family Home
*Humayan Place, near New Market.*
Excellent Indian vegetarian meals, particularly recommended for South Indian, good *lassis*, cheap and busy.

### $ Fresh and Juicy
*Chowringhee Lane, T033-2286 1638.*
Recently renovated with a/c and 1st floor seating, good place for a sociable breakfast or reasonably authentic Indian meals and Western favourites, attracts a loyal following. Phone ahead for parcel-order.

### $ Khalsa
*4C Madge Lane, T033-2249 0075.*
Excellent *lassis*, Western breakfasts, Indian mains, all super-cheap, and with excellent service from the utterly charming Sikh owners.

## $ Maya Ram
*1 Lord Sinha Rd. Open 1100-2300.*
A good place to try 'snacks' such as
*paw bhaji.*

## $ Momo Plaza
*2A Suburban Hospital Rd. Open 1200-2200.*
With black half-tiling and pastel pink
walls accentuated by kitsch ornaments,
which could be intentionally bohemian.
Recommended for plentiful and delicious
Tibetan and Chinese meals. Try the soups,
chilli chicken, huge *momos* and *thukpa.*
Nearby $ **Hamro Momo** is also good,
cheaper and more crowded.

## $ NV Stores and Maa Kali
*12/2 Lindsay St. Closed Sun.*
Stand-up street eateries making surprisingly
good sandwiches (toasted are best) from
any possible combination of ingredients;
great *lassis* too.

## $ Raj's Spanish Café
*7 Sudder St. Daily 0800-2200.*
Spanish nibbles, real coffee from a real
machine, salads, pastries, pasta and
sandwiches also good. Wi-Fi. A sociable spot.

## $ Tirupati
*Street stall next to Hotel Maria.*
A Sudder St institution; find a spot on the
busy benches and enjoy enormous helpings
of food from every continent.

### Coffee shops, sweets and snacks

### Ashalayam
*44 Mirza Ghalib St.*
Peaceful oasis run by an NGO, sells
handicrafts made by street children
as well as coffee and snacks.

### Brothers Snacks
*1 Humayun Pl, Newmarket.*
Safe, tasty bet with outdoor seats. Kati
rolls (tender kebabs, or paneer, or egg/
vegetables, wrapped in *parathas*) are hard
to beat. Try mutton/chicken egg roll (if you

don't want raw onions and green chillis,
order *'no piaaz e mirchi'*) There are also plenty
of great vegetarian options.

### Café Thé
*Tagore Centre, 9A Ho Chi Min Sarani.*
*Daily 0900-2100.*
Modern, clean cafe serving Western/Indian/
Chinese snacks and meals, with
an interesting menu of hot/cold teas.

### Kathleen's
*Several branches, including 12 Mirza Ghalib*
*St, corner of Lord Sinha Rd.*

### Nahoum's
*Shop F20, New Market.*
Good pastries, cakes, savouries and brown
bread. The original 1930s till and some
fixtures still in situ.

### Pure Milk Centre
*Near Rafi Ahmed Kidwai St/Ripon St corner.*
Good sweet 'curd' (*mishti doi*), usually sold
out by lunchtime. Excellent hot *roshogollas.*

### Rehmania and Shiraz Golden Restaurant
*On opposite corners of Park St/*
*AJC Bose Rd crossing.*
Muslim joints famed for their mutton rolls
and kebabs.

---

### South Kolkata

### $$$ Chinoiserie
*Taj Bengal (see Where to stay, page 48),*
*T033-2223 3939.*
Good for a splurge on excellent Chinese.

### $$$ Mainland China
*3A Gurusaday Rd, T033-2283 7964;*
*also at South City Mall, 3rd floor.*
Sublime Chinese. Unusual offerings,
especially fish and seafood, tastefully
decorated with burnished ceiling and
evocative wall mural, pleasant ambience,
courteous. Book ahead.

### $$$ Oh! Calcutta
*In the Forum Mall, 10/3 Elgin Rd, T033-2283 7161.*
Fantastic fish and seafood, plus many vegetarian options, this award-winning restaurant (branches across India, another in Kolkata on EM Bypass) re-creates Bengali specialties. It's an attractive venue, although located inside a mall.

### $$$-$$ 6 Ballygunge Place
*Ballygunge, T033-2460 3922.*
In a charming Raj-era bungalow, the intricate Bengali menu is as delightful as the ambiance. For more than a decade, this has been the perfect place for a special night out. Again, the fish dishes are a highlight.

### $$ Kewpie's
*2 Elgin Lane (just off Elgin Rd), T033-2486 1600/9929. Tue-Sun 1200-1500, 1700-2245.*
Authentic Bengali home cooking at its best, add on special dishes to basic *thali*, unusual fish and vegetarian. Just a few tables in rooms inside the owners' residence, a/c, sells recipe book.

### $$ Krystal Chopsticks
*71H Hindustan Park. Open 1200-2230.*
Attractive East Asian decor and an excellent menu (chiefly Chinese) attracts well-heeled Bengalis. It's not outrageously priced, plenty of interesting vegetarian as well as chicken, fish and meat dishes.

### $$ Mirch Masala
*49/2 Gariahat Rd, Gariahat, T033-2461 8900. Lunch 1200-1500, dinner 1900-2230.*
This popular restaurant-bar has walls decorated with *pukkah* murals depicting Bollywood stars. Food can be a bit heavy (mainly Indian, non-veg), but the atmosphere is lively and staff competent.

### $$-$ Bhojohori Manna
*13 PC Sorcar Sarani (aka Ekdalia Rd); also at JD Park.*
Budget prices and a perfect little place to sample pure Bengali cuisine, veg and

non-veg. Ticks on the wall menu indicate availability, try *echor dalna* (jackfruit curry) and *bhekti paturi* (mustard-drenched fish steamed in banana leaves). 2 people should order 4-5 different dishes to share. Much better than the newer **Bhojohori 6** outlet on Hindustan Rd nearby. Decent toilet.

### $ Banana Leaf
*73-75 Rash Behari Av. Open 0730-2200.*
Vegetarian South Indian, top-notch *dosas* and *thalis* plus superb *mini-iddli* and decent southern-style coffee.

### $ Bliss
*53 Hindustan Park.*
For Chinese in a fast-food environment, Bliss is ideal. Portions are generous, the soups delicious. It's tiny but there's seating.

### $ South India Club
*Off Rash Behari Av. Daily 0700-2130.*
An authentic taste of the South in a canteen environment, full meals for under Rs 50, and a good place to experiment with less commonly seen dishes such as *pongal* or *upma*.

## Coffee shops, sweets and snacks

### Art Café
*At The Bodhi Tree (see Where to stay, page 49). Tue-Sat, 1400-1830.*
Half-inside/half-outside, this beautiful slate-floored café is lit by green lights and decorated with Buddhas, palm trees and original works of art (exhibitions are occasionally held). There's a tempting drinks menu (plus beer) in addition to light meals. Something quite out of the ordinary for Kolkata.

### Dolly's The Tea Shop
*Dakshinapan market (just after Dhakuria Bridge).*
The quaintest place in the city for a variety of teas, refreshing iced-teas (try watermelon) and decent toasties. Tea-chest tables, low

basket chairs, indoor and outdoor seating, even the walls are lined with old tea-crates. Dolly is a formidable lady.

### Nepal Sweets
*16B Sarat Bose Rd.*
*Chandrakala*, almond *pista barfi*, mango *roshogolla*, *kheer mohan* (also savouries). Recommended.

### Other areas
Chinese food fans also go to South Tangra Rd off EM bypass, east of the city centre. The approach is none too picturesque, past tanneries and open drains, but among the maze of lanes (in places lit by lanterns) many eateries are quite swanky.

**$$ Beijing**
*77/1A Christopher Rd, T033-2328 1001.*
Try garlic chicken, sweet and sour fish, chop suey, steamed fish, generous portions.

**$$ Golden Joy, Kafulok** and **Sin Fa**, to name but a few, offer excellent soups, jumbo prawns and honey chicken, best to go early (1200 for lunch, 2000 for dinner).

## Bars and clubs

The larger hotels have pleasant bars and upmarket restaurants serve alcohol. The top hotels are well stocked, luxurious but pricey. 'Local' bars are usually open 1100-2230, often lack atmosphere or have deafening live singing; some are for men only; there is a seedy choice down Dacres Lane, just north of Esplanade.

### Central Kolkata

#### Broadway Bar
*At the Broadway Hotel (last orders 2230), see Where to stay.*
Has marble floors, polished Art Deco seating, soft lighting, whirring fans and windows open to the street, making it probably the best choice in the city. Lone women will feel

comfortable as it's a busy and respectable place. For a sunset drink on the water, try the **Floatel**, a floating hotel on the Hooghly moored close to Babu Ghat. The simple bar is usually quiet, and has a small outdoor area, good for watching the river life.

### Park Street, Chowringhee and Sudder Street
**Fairlawn's** pleasant garden terrace is popular at dusk attracting anyone seeking a chilled beer. The clientele is mixed, fairy lights set the greenery glowing and it's perfect for a 1st night drink to acclimatize – but beware the below-average food and stiff charges for snacks. **Super Pub Bar** (Sudder St), is always busy and sociable, but expect gruff service and check your change. **Blue & Beyond** (at the **Lindsay Hotel**) is a rooftop bar/restaurant with great views over Kolkata from the 9th-floor (quite pricey), plus an indoor a/c section. The bar at the **New Empire Cinema** (between New Market and Chowringhee), is pleasant, blue-lit and efficiently staffed. **Sam's Pub** (off Park St, is open later than most, last orders at 2330 on weekend nights) and still permits smoking in a curious indoor gazebo; football and cricket matches are shown on the flatscreen. **Oly Pub** (21 Park St), is an institution: very noisy, serves steak and eggs, more airy downstairs. At **Someplace Else** (**Park Hotel**), live bands play loud music to the same crowd each week. **Tantra** (also in **Park Hotel**) has taped music, large dancefloor, young crowd, no shorts or flip-flops, cover charge. Next door, **Roxy** is less popular, but has free entry and is more relaxed, with slouchy sofas upstairs. **Shisha Reincarnated** (Block D, 6th floor, 22 Camac St, www. shishareincarnated.com, open 1800-2400, Wed, Fri and Sat 1800-0200) is dark and stylish, with a chilled atmosphere, low red lights, a huge bar lined with spirits, DJs every night (varying music styles) and a decent

sized dancefloor. Hookahs available. The roof-deck is the best place to hang out.

## South Kolkata

**Tripti's** (SP Mukerjee Rd (next to Netaji Bhavan metro), Mon-Sat 1100-2300, Sun 1100-2200), is a classic. Established in 1935 and styled like a canteen, it's been tackily refurnished, but the 1950s flooring and shuttered windows remain. Expect rowdiness and cheap booze. On the 1st floor up hidden steps; look for the sign. Take a wander round sprawling and atmospheric **Jadu Babu Bazar** to the rear while in the area. Also here is pub/club **The Basement** (**Samilton Hotel**, 35A Sarat Bose Rd), where you can hear a variety of live music (Wed-Fri); there's also a shisha place on the rooftop. **Underground** (at the **Hindusthan International**) has good music and a young crowd; it's a long-stayer on the scene. The noisy dance-bar beneath **Ginger** restaurant (106 SP Mukerjee Rd, T033-2486 3052/3, near JD Park metro) accommodates same-sex couples, open 1130-2330.

## Entertainment

The English-language dailies (*Telegraph*, *Times of India*, etc) carry a comprehensive list.

### Art galleries

**Academy of Fine Arts**, *Cathedral Rd (see page 31)*.

**Ahuja Museum for Arts**, *26 Lee Rd (Elgin Rd crossing with AJC Bose), www.ahujaptm.com/ museum*. The private collection of Mr SD Ahuja contains over 1200 works of art, which are displayed in rotation.

**Bengal Gallery**, *Rabindranath Tagore Centre, 9A Ho Chi Min Sarani*. The Indian Council for Cultural Relations has a large space showing established artists.

**Chemould Art Gallery**, *12F Park St*. One of the big names in contemporary art, and worth keeping an eye on.

**CIMA**, *2nd floor, Sunny Towers, 43 Ashutosh Chowdhury Av, www.cimaartindia.com. Tue-Sat 1100-1900, closed Sun, Mon 1500-1900*. The best exhibition space in the city and the shop has a good stock in wall-hangings, metalwork, clothes, stoles, ornaments, etc.

**Experimenter**, *2/1 Hindustan Rd, Gariahat*. A trendy contemporary space with great exhibitions by Indian and international artists.

**Harrington Street Arts Centre**, *2nd Floor, 8 Ho Chi Minh Sarani, http://hstreetarts centre.com*. Cool white space in an old apartment, hosting quality photography and art exhibitions.

**Seagull Arts and Media Centre**, *36C SP Mukherjee Rd (just off Mukherjee on a sidestreet), www.seagullindia.com*. Holds regular photography exhibitions from 1400-2000. Also has a bookshop on the opposite side of SP Mukherjee.

**Studio 21**, *17/L Dover Terrace (off Ballygunge Phari), www.studio21kolkata.com*. A minimalist new space for emerging artists from all disciplines, art/photography exhibitions change regularly.

### Cinema

A/c and comfortable cinemas showing English-language films are a good escape from the heat, and many are still very cheap. Check the newspapers for timings; programmes change every Fri. **Elite** (SN Banerjee Rd), and **New Empire Cinema** (New Market St) are conveniently close to Sudder St. **Nandan Complex** (AJC Bose Rd) shows classics and art house movies; the **Kolkata International Film Festival** is held here in Nov, an excellent event. Swish **Inox** multiplexes (www.inoxmovies.com) are scattered around town (Forum, City Centre); tickets for these can be booked by credit card over the phone. **Fame cinema** (www. famecinemas.com) in South City Mall, is open 1000-0100.

## Performing arts

There are regular performances at **Rabindra Sadan** (Cathedral Rd); the adjacent **Sisir Mancha has Bengali theatre. Kala Mandir** (48 Shakespeare Sarani), has regular cultural performances, Rabindranath Tagore Centre (9A Ho Chi Min Sarani, www.tagorecentre iccr.org) has a lovely new concert hall. You can also see Bengali theatre of a high standard at **Biswaroopa** (2A Raja Raj Kissen St) and **Star Theatre** (79/34 Bidhan Sarani). English-language productions are staged by the British Council and theatre clubs. **Sangeet Research Academy** (www.itcsra.org), near Mahanayak Uttam (Tollygunge) Metro station, is a national centre for training in Indian classical music and stages a free concert on Wed evenings. **Rabindra Bharati University** (6/4 Dwarakanath Tagore Lane) holds performances, particularly during the winter, including singing, dancing and *jatras*.

## Festivals

**Jan Ganga Sagar Mela** at Sagardwip, 105 km south of Kolkata, where the River Hooghly joins the sea, draws thousands of Hindu pilgrims. See page 62.

**Apr Bengali New Year (Poila Baiskh)** is celebrated around 15 Apr.

**Jun-Jul Ratha Yatra** at Mahesh, near Serampur, Hooghly District. Week-long chariot festival.

**Sep-Oct Durga Puja**, Bengal's celebration of the goddess during **Dasara**. See box, page 39.

**Oct-Nov** *Kali Puja* is the 1-day festival of lights.

**Dec Christmas**. Many churches hold special services, including Midnight Mass, and the New Market takes on a new look in Dec as **Barra Din** (Big Day) approaches with stalls selling trees and baubles. Other religious festivals are observed as elsewhere in India.

## Shopping

Most shops open Mon-Sat 1000-1730 or later (some break for lunch). New Market stalls, and most shops, close on Sun.

### Books

**College St**, a thicket of second-hand pavement bookstalls along this street. They're mainly for students, but may reveal an interesting 1st edition for a keen collector (see page 35).

**Crossword**, *Elgin Rd.* Deservedly popular chain store, with 2 floors of books, films, good selection of magazines and films and a busy coffee shop.

**Earthcare Books**, *10 Middleton St (by Drive Inn), T033-2229 6551, www.earth carebooks.com*. Excellent selection of children's books, Indian-focussed titles, socially conscious books, plenty of fiction, has small photo exhibitions.

**Family Book Shop**, *1A Park St.* Good selection of guidebooks. 10-15% discounts possible.

**Kolkata Book Fair**, *Milan Mela Prangan, EM Bypass, www.kolkatabookfair.net*. End of Jan for a fortnight, stalls sell paperback fiction to antiquarian books.

**Mirza Ghalib St.** Has a string of small shops selling new, used and photocopied versions of current favourites. Bargaining required.

**Oxford Book Shop**, *Park St.* Huge selection of English titles, postcards and films, café upstairs where you can browse through titles. Excellent for books on Kolkata, and a children's bookshop next door.

## Bengali crafts

Silk has been woven in India for more than 3500 years and continues today with the weaving of natural-coloured wild silk called *tassar*. Bengal silk has had a revival in the exquisite brocade weaving of *baluchari* saris, produced in the past under royal patronage and now carried out in Bankura. The saris are woven in traditional style with untwisted silk and have beautiful borders and *pallu* decorations, depicting peacocks, flowers and human figures. Fine cotton is also woven.

The Bankura horse has become a symbol of West Bengali pottery, which is still produced in the districts of Bankura, Midnapore and Birbhum. Soft soap stone is used for carving copies of temple images, while shell bangles are considered auspicious. Ivory carvers once produced superb decorative items, a skill developed in the Mughal period; today, bone and plastic have largely replaced ivory in inlay work. Metal workers produce brass and bell metalware, while the tribal *dhokra* casters still follow the ancient *cire perdue* method. Kalighat *pat* paintings are in a primitive style using bold colours.

**Seagull**, *31A SP Mukherjee Rd, www.seagull india.com*. Large and unusual stock of art-related books, coffee-table tomes, etc.
**Starmark**, *top floor, Emami Centre, 3 Lord Sinha Rd; also City Centre and South City Mall.* The best selection of fiction in Kolkata, plus imported magazines, films.

### Clothes and accessories
**Anokhi**, *Shop 209, Forum Shopping Mall, 10/3 Lala Lajpat Rai Sarani, near AJC Bose Rd.* Beautiful block-print bed-linens, floaty bed-wear, scarves, accessories, clothes and more. Made in Jaipur, mid-range prices.
**Biba**, *South City Mall, Prince Anwar Shar Rd, www.bibaindia.com*; also has franchises in **Pantaloons** department stores. Chic cotton print dresses, tasteful *salwar*.
**Fabindia**, *16 Hindustan Park (also branches at Woodburn Park Rd, near AJC Bose Rd, and City Centre Mall in Salt Lake).* Clothes, textiles, toiletries, rugs and home furnishings from fair-trade company. Hugely successful due to their tasteful and high-quality selection. Well worth a visit.

**Gomukh**, *next to Raj's Spanish Café, 7 Sudder St.* Traveller wear, plus a range of scarves and wall-hangings, cheap and well stocked.
**Khazana**, *Taj Bengal (see Where to stay, page 48).* For pricey textiles, Baluchari saris, *kantha* embroidery, etc, and souvenirs.

### Government emporia
Government emporia are mainly in the town centre and are fixed-price shops. All the Indian states are represented at **Dakshinapan** (near Dhakuria Bridge, Mon-Fri 1030-1930, Sat 1030-1400), which has an excellent selection of handloom and handicrafts.
**Central Cottage Industries** (7 JL Nehru Rd), is convenient as is **Kashmir Art** (12 JL Nehru Rd).
**Phulkari** (Punjab Emporium, 26B Camac St).
**Rajasthali** (30E JL Nehru Rd). **Tripura** (58 JL Nehru Rd). **UP** (12B Lindsay St).

### Handicrafts and handloom
There are many handicraft shops around Newmarket St, selling batik prints, handloom, blockprints and embroidery, but starting prices are usually excessive so bargain hard. Shops listed below are all either fair trade-based or associated with self-help groups.

**Artisana**, *13 Chowringhee Pl (off Gokhale Rd), T033-2223 9422*. Handloom and handicrafts, traditional hand-block textiles, designer jewellery, metalware and more.

**Ashalayam Handicrafts**, *1st floor, 44 Mirza Ghalib St*. Products made by street children who have been trained and given shelter by the **Don Bosco Ashalayam Project**. Proceeds are split between the artisans and the trust.

**Bengal Home Industries Association**, *11 Camac St*. Good selection of printed cotton (bedspreads, saris) and assorted knick-knacks. Relaxed, fixed price.

**Calcutta Rescue Handicrafts**, *Fairlawn Hotel. Thu 1830*. Medical NGO sells great selection of cards, bags and trinkets made and embroidered by former patients.

**Kamala**, *1st floor, Tagore Centre, 9A Ho Chi Min Sarani*. Outlet shop for the Crafts Council of West Bengal; great selection of textiles, jewellery, gifts and trinkets at very reasonable prices (sourced directly from the artisans).

**Karmyog**, *12B Russell St*. Gorgeous handcrafted paper products.

**Sasha**, *27 Mirza Ghalib St, www.sasha world.com*. Attractive range of good-quality, fair-trade textiles, furnishings, ceramics, metalwork, etc, but not cheap, welcome a/c.

### Jewellery

**Bepin Behari Ganguly St** (Bow Bazar) is lined with mirrored jewellers' shops; **PC Chandra, BB Dutt, B Sirkar** are well known. Also many on Rash Behari Av. The **silver market** (*rupa bajar*) is off Mirza Ghalib St opposite Newmarket. Gold and silver prices are listed daily in the newspapers.

### Markets

The **New Market**, Lindsay St, has more than 2500 shops (many closed Sun). You will find mundane everyday necessities and exotic luxuries, from fragrant florists to gory meat stalls. Be prepared to deal with pestering basket-wallahs.

Kolkata has a number of bazars, each with a character of its own. In **Bentinck St** are Muslim tailors, Chinese shoemakers plus Indian sweetmeat shops and tea stalls. **Gariahat market** early in the morning attracts a diverse clientele (businessmen, academics, cooks) who come to select choice fresh fish. In **Shyambazar** the coconut market lasts from 0500 to 0700. **Burra Bazar** is a hectic wholesale fruit market held daily. The colourful **flower market** is on Jagannath Ghat on the river bank. The old **China Bazar** no longer exists although **Tiretta Bazar** area still retains its ethnic flavour; try an exceptional Chinese breakfast from a street stall.

### Musical instruments

**Braganza's**, *56C Free School (Mirza Ghalib) St*. An institution; with an extensive collection. Also head to the southern end of Rabindra Sarani for musical instruments (sitars, tablas, etc).

### Tailors

Garments can be skillfully copied around New Market and on Madge Lane. Tailors will try to overcharge foreigners as a matter of course.

What to do

### Body and soul

Look out for adverts around Sudder St for yoga classes held on hotel rooftops.

**Aurobindo Bhavan**, *8 Shakespeare Sarani, www.sriaurobindobhavankolkata.org*. Very informal yoga classes, women on Mon/Wed/Fri 1530-1930, men on Tue/Thu/Sat 1530-1930 (Rs 200). Bring a copy of your passport and visa.

**Mystic Yoga**, *20/A Camac St, www.mystic yoga.in*. Drop-in classes Rs 300, or monthly memberships, healthy café on site.

## Cricket

Occasional Test matches and One-Day Internationals and regular IPL fixtures at Eden Gardens, see page 29, 100,000 capacity.

## Golf

**Royal Calcutta Golf Club**, *18 Golf Club Rd, www.rcgc.in*. Founded in 1829, the oldest golf club in the world outside the UK.
**The Tollygunge Club**, *120 Despran Sasmal Rd, www.tollygungeclub.org*. The course is on land that was once an indigo plantation.

## Horse racing

At the southern end of the Maidan is **Kolkata Race Course**, run by the Royal Calcutta Turf Club, www.rctconline.com. The history of racing goes back to the time of Warren Hastings, and the 1820s grandstand is especially impressive. Racing takes place in the cool season (Nov to early Apr) and monsoon season (Jul-Oct). The Derby is in the 1st week of Jan. It's a fun, cheap day out in the public stands, better still if you can access the members' enclosure to get up close to the racehorses and enjoy a drink in the bar with antlers mounted on the wall.

## Heritage tours

To really appreciate the architecture and culture of the city in the company of expert guides, get in touch with one of the organizations listed below. Tours generally last 2-4 hrs.
**Calcutta Photo Tours**, *www.calcuttaphoto tours.com*. Combining sightseeing with photography tips, and covering a diverse range of topics and districts.
**Calcutta Walks**, *http://calcuttawalks.com*. Themes include food, colonial history, markets and motorbike tours, with engaging guides.
**Walks of Calcutta**, *www.walksofkolkata.com*. Uncovers more hidden treasures in the city.

## Sightseeing tours

**WBTDC**, *departure point is Tourism Centre, 3/2 BBD Bagh E, 1st floor, T033-2248 8271*.
*Daily tours, 0830-1730*. Tour stops at: Eden Gardens, High Court, Writers' Building, Belur Math, Dakshineswar Kali Temple, Jain Temple, Netaji Bhavan, Kolkata Panorama and Esplanade, Victoria Memorial, St Paul's Cathedral and Kali Ghat. Entry fees not included. Approved guides from **Govt of India Tourist Office**, T033-2582 5813.

## Swimming

**Wet 'O' Wild**, *at Nicco Park, HM Block, Salt Lake City, http://niccoparks.com/wet-o-wild*. Kolkata's best waterpark with a truly enormous pool and wave machine. The **Hindusthan International Hotel** pool is open to non-residents for a fee.

## Tour operators

Deals in air tickets to/from the East (through Bangkok) are offered by agents in the Sudder St area, or book online.
**Help Tourism**, *Sadananda Kothi (1st floor), 67A Kali Temple Rd, Kalighat, www.help tourism.com*. Wide variety of wildlife and adventure tours in Assam, Arunachal and North Bengal, with strong eco credentials and involvement of local communities.

## Volunteer work

Many people come to Kolkata to work with one of the many NGOs. The following organizations accept volunteers, though it's wise to contact them in advance (except for the **Missionaries of Charity**, where you only need to attend one of the registration days).
**Don Bosco Ashalayam Project**, *www. dbasha.org*. Rehabilitates young homeless people by teaching skills.
**Hope Kolkata Foundation**, *39 Panditya Pl, www.hopechild.org*. An Irish charity focussing on the needs of disadvantaged children.
**Missionaries of Charity (Mother Teresa)**, *The Mother House, 54A AJC Bose Rd, T033-2249 7115*. The majority of volunteers work at one of the Mother Teresa homes. Induction/registration sessions are at 1500 on Mon, Wed and Fri in various languages.

## Transport

**Air** The large terminals of Nataji Subhas Chandra Bose airport are well organized and have been recently renovated. A reservation counter for rail (same-day travel only) is found in the Arrivals hall. There are money changers by the exit of the terminal and a taxi booth.

**Transport to the city** Taxis take 45-60 mins and cost about Rs 400 (deluxe cars Rs 600-800); there is a prepaid taxi booth at Arrivals. A/c buses are available from outside Terminal 1 Arrivals; some go to Howrah (via the city centre) and Esplanade (from where it is a 15-min walk to Sudder St), taking at least 1 hr and costing about Rs 50. They also go to Tollygunge. A bus/metro combination is not recommended for new arrivals as it requires a 400-m walk across the car park to the main road, and then changing to the nearest Metro station at Dum Dum; auto-rickshaws to the Metro cost about Rs 100.

**Bicycle** Bike hire is not easy; ask at your hotel if a staff bike is free. Spares are sold along Bentinck St, north of Chowringhee.

**Bus Local** State transport services run throughout the city and suburbs from 0500-2030; usually overcrowded after 0830, but very cheap (the big blue-yellow buses are noteworthy for their artwork) and a good way to get around. Maroon minibuses (little more expensive) also cover major routes. Newer a/c buses are becoming commonplace.

**Long distance** Long-distance buses use the Esplanade depot, 15 mins' walk from Sudder St. Advance bookings are made at the computerized office of **Calcutta State Transport Corp (CSTC)**, Esplanade, T033-2248 1916. To **Digha** 0530-1600; **Malda**; **Siliguri** (12 hrs); **Bishnupur** and other towns in West Bengal. More comfortable private a/c buses with push-back seats to Siliguri also depart from Esplanade; good are **Royal Cruisers**, T(0)9903-400926. **Odisha & Bihar STC**, Babu Ghat: to **Ranchi**; **Dhaka**, **Gaya**, **Puri** (11 hrs). **Bhutan Govt**, to **Phuntsholing** via **Siliguri**, 1900, 16 hrs.

**To Bangladesh** Private buses to **Dhaka** can be booked from numerous agencies on Marquis St, from where they also depart.

**Ferry Local** To cross the Hooghly, between Howrah station and Babu Ghat, Rs 5, except Sun. During festivals a ferry goes from Babu Ghat to Belur Math, 1 hr.

**Long distance** Shipping Corp of India, 1st floor, 13 Strand Rd (enter from Hare St), T033-2248 4921, 1000-1300 (for tickets), 1400-1745 (information only), see schedules at www.andamantourism.in/shipschedule. html, operates a steamer to **Port Blair** in the Andamans. Some 2 or 3 sailings a month (66 hrs), Rs 1961-7631 one way. For tickets go 4 days in advance, and be there by 0830; huge queue for 'bunk class'.

**Metro** The recently extended Metro line runs for 25 km from Dum Dum in the north to Kavi Subhash in the south, every 7-12 mins Mon-Sat 0700-2145, Sun 1400-2145; fare Rs 5-25. Note that Tollygunge has been renamed 'Mahanayak Uttam Kumar' on station signs, but is still commonly referred to as Tollygunge. There are women-only sections interspersed throughout the train. A further 5 metro lines are planned for the future.

**Rickshaw** Hand-pulled rickshaws are used by locals along the narrow congested lanes. Auto-rickshaws operate outside the city centre, especially as shuttle service to/from Metro stations along set routes. Auto-rickshaws from Sealdah station to Sudder St cost about Rs 80.

**Taxi** Tourist taxis are available from **India Tourism** and **WBTDC** offices. Local taxis are yellow Ambassadors: insist on the meter, then use conversion chart to calculate correct fare.

## BORDER CROSSING
### To Bangladesh

**Petrapol–Benapol**
This crossing is the most reliable as a visa on arrival is available at the Bangladeshi border for nationals of many countries (including USA, EU and Australia). The 30-day single entry visa costs US$51.

There are direct private buses from Kolkata to Dhaka, which can be booked through travel agencies on Marquis Street. Alternatively, take a train from Sealdah to Bangaon railway station (two hours) from where buses and minibuses go to the border at Petrapol. On the Bangladesh side, buses (seven hours to Dhaka) and rickshaws are available. The *Maintree Express* train (11 hours) from Kolkata through to Dhaka uses a different border crossing, and travellers report not being issued a visa on arrival here (and having to backtrack to Petrapol). If you wish to take the *Maintree Express*, arrange a visa in advance from your home country. However, regulations are subject to change, so check the latest situation at http://visitbangladesh.gov.bd/travel-essentials/visa-service.

**Train** Kolkata is served by 2 main railway stations, **Howrah** (enquiries, T033-2638 7412/3542) and **Sealdah** (T033-2350 3535). Howrah station has a separate complex for platforms 18-21 (T033-2660 2217). Foreign tourist quota tickets are sold at both stations until 1400, at which point tickets go on general sale. Railway reservations can be made at Fairlie Place, BBD Bagh, Mon-Sat 1000-1300, 1330-1700, Sun 1000-1400 (best to go early). Tourists are automatically told to go to the Foreign Tourist Counter to get Foreign Tourist Quota; it takes 10-30 mins; you will need to show your passport and complete a reservation form; payment in rupees is accepted.

Trains listed depart from Howrah (**H**), unless marked '(**S**)' for Sealdah. **Agra Fort**: at least 6 per day, around 20 hrs. **Bhubaneswar** and on to **Puri**: over 10 per day, 6-7 hrs. **Chennai**: at least 2 per day, 28 hrs. **Mumbai**: at least 4 per day, 27-38 hrs, via **Nagpur** (18 hrs) or **Gaya** (7½ hrs); at least 5 per day to **New Delhi** via **Gaya** and **Allahabad**, or **Patna**, between 17-27 hrs. **New Jalpaiguri** (**NJP**): at least 10 per day, by far the best is the *Darjeeling Mail 12343*, leaving from Sealdah at 2205, 10 hrs. **Ranchi**: best is *Howrah Shatabdi Exp 12019*, 0605 (except Sun), 7 hrs.

**To Bangladesh** It is possible to travel direct to **Dhaka** on the *Maitree Express* from **Chitpur Terminal**, twice weekly, 0710, 11 hrs.

**Tram** Kolkata is the only Indian city to run a tram network. Many trams originate at **Esplanade depot** and it's a great way to see the city: ride route 1 to Belgachia through the heart of North Kolkata's heritage, or route 36 to Kidderpore through the Maidan. Route 26 goes from the **Gariahat depot** in the south all the way to Howrah, via Sealdah and College St. Services run 0430-2230, with a restricted service at the weekends.

# South
## of Kolkata

To the south of Kolkata are the tidal estuary of the Hooghly and the mangrove forests of the Sundarbans, which reach into Bangladesh and are famous for their population of Bengal tigers. It's possible to take a day trip down to the mouth of the Hooghly or a boat trip into the Sundarbans themselves: a magical experience through gorgeous scenery, although tiger sightings are rare.

### Sagardwip Island

The **Ganga Sagar Mela** festival is held in mid-January, attracting over 500,000 pilgrims each year who come to bathe and then visit the **Kapil Muni Temple**. The island has been devastated many times by cyclones. To get there catch a bus from Esplanade or take a taxi to Kakdwip and then take a ferry across to Kochuberia Ghat (Sagardwip). From there it is a 30-minute bus ride across the island to where the Ganga meets the sea by the temple.

### Digha

Digha was described by Warren Hastings visiting in 1780 as the 'Brighton of the East', though there is not a pebble for at least 2000 km. The casuarina-lined, firm wide beach is popular with Bengalis and hotels are clustered around one main road. The small **Chandaneswar Temple**, 9 km away, actually in Odisha, is an important Siva temple which can be reached by bus.

Sunderbans (pronounced Shunder-bon) is named after the Sunderi trees and literally means 'a beautiful forest'. The mangrove swamps are said to be the largest estuarine forests in the world.

The reserve, a UNESCO World Heritage Site, preserves the habitat of about 300 Bengal tigers (*Panthera tigris*). They are bigger and richer in colour than elsewhere in South Asia and are thought to be able to survive on salt water (rainwater is the only fresh water in the park). Tigers here are strong swimmers and known to attack fishermen.

Most villagers depend on fishing and forestry, although local honey gatherers are active in April and May. (They are said to wear masks on the backs of their heads to frighten away tigers, which they believe only attack from the rear!) You will notice large areas of *bheries* for aquaculture. Prawn fisheries are the most lucrative, and co-operative efforts are being encouraged by the government. Improved management is battling to halt the loss of mangrove cover, which is exploited for fuel, and to provide permanent sources of fresh water for the tigers by digging deep, monsoon-fed ponds and installing solar-powered lighting to scare them away from villages.

## Essential Sunderbans Tiger Reserve

### Permits

A permit is required to visit the reserve for a maximum of five days (Rs 150 for foreigners). If you're travelling independently, permits are available from **WBTDC** in Kolkata (see page 45); take your passport. Alternatively, you can get them on arrival at the **Forest Department Office** in Sajnekhali Wildlife Sanctuary. In addition to the cost of the permit, you need to pay fees of Rs 200 for a guide, Rs 100 for a boat and Rs 300 for video cameras. It is much easier to visit on a tour when all permits, transport and accommodation will be organized for you.

### Getting around

Motor launches can be hired from Canning and Sonakhali (Basanti), but it is better to go down the narrow creeks in human-powered boats. You may be able to go ashore on bamboo jetties to walk in the fenced-in areas of the forest which have watchtowers (dawn to dusk only). You must

### Tip...
Amitv Ghosh's *The Hungry Tide* is the perfect read when exploring the islands and waterways of the Sunderbans.

be accompanied by armed forest rangers. Since these are tidal waterways, boats are not always able to moor near the ghats, and during monsoons or bad weather they will not sail.

### When to go

The best season is October to March. Heavy rains and occasional cyclones in April/May and November/December can make visiting difficult at these times. Avoid visiting the Sunderbans at weekends, when the reserve is very busy with domestic tourists.

### What to bring

Take drinking water, a torch and mosquito repellent, and be prepared for cool nights.

Although you are unlikely to see a tiger, there are spotted deer, wild boar, monkeys, snakes, fishing cats, water monitors, olive ridley sea turtles and a few large estuarine crocodiles here, particularly on Lothian Island and Chamta block.

## Listings South of Kolkata

### Tourist information

**Sunderbans Tiger Reserve**

West Bengal Tourism Development Corporation (WBTDC)
*2/3 BBD Bagh East, T033-2248 8271, www.wbtourism.gov.in. Mon-Fri 1030-1630, Sat 1030-1300; also a counter at the station in Howrah.*
A more useful office with plenty of staff and brochures; you can get a permit for the Sunderbans from here (bring passports).

### Where to stay

**Sagardwip**
**WBTDC** runs expensive 2-day boat trips with lodging on board during **Ganga Sagar Mela**, including a/c coach. You can also stay at the *dharamshala* for a donation.

**$ Youth Hostel**
*Book via the Youth Services office in Kolkata, T033-2248 0626, ext 27.*

**Digha**
There is plenty of choice close to the beach to suit all budgets.

**$$ Sea Coast**
*T032-2026 6305, www.hotelseacoast.com.*
With some a/c rooms, this is the best 3-star option.

**$$-$ Tourist Lodge**
*T032-2026 6255.*
Rooms on 3 floors, some a/c, dorm, bar, restaurant.

**Sunderbans Tiger Reserve**
A few basic lodges are found in Gosaba. There is also one in Pakhirala, the last village before Sajnekhali.

**$$$$ Vivada Cruises**
*T1-800 345 0088, www.sunderbancruises.com.*
The first luxury cruise boat to be launched on this route, eco-friendly with 32 rooms, internet, open-air gym, sauna, sunbathing deck and multicuisine restaurants. Package for 3 days/4 nights, or 7 days/8 nights including meals and excursions.

**$$$-$$ Sunderbans Jungle Camp**
*Bali village; book through Help Tourism in Kolkata, www.helptourism.com.*
Indigenous-style bungalows with modern bathrooms, in a community tourism venture set up by a group of ex-poachers. Local fishermen supply fish and offer trips into mangrove forests; it's also a chance to interact with villagers and experience authentic folk performances. Book as a package, all meals included (open-air restaurant), prices go down the more members in your group.

**$$$-$$ Sunderban Tiger Camp**
*Dayapur Island, T033-3293 5749, www.sunderbantigercamp.com.*
'Tents' with thatched roofs, huts, mud cottages and a/c cottages, in a peaceful location with nice gardens. Village walks and fishing trips, as well as tours on comfortable boats. Restaurant serves range of cuisines and seafood, there's a bar and a library. Price includes transport from Kolkata.

## $ Tourist Lodge
*Sajnekhali, contact through WBTDC, T03218-214960, www.wbtdc.gov.in.*
Raised on pillars and fenced from wildlife, solar power, small basic rooms with mosquito nets, hot water in buckets, 20-bed dorm, simple meals (price includes breakfast and 1 meal). Book ahead; permits can be arranged at the Forest Office on site.

## What to do

### Sunderbans Tiger Reserve
**Help Tourism**, *Kolkata (see page 59).* Excellent community-based tours and has a camp near the reserve (see Where to Stay, above).
**WBTDC Tours**: 2-day and 3-day trips (infrequent during monsoon, Jul-Sep), by coach from Kolkata then 'luxury' launch with onboard accommodation. Prices vary between vessels and with standard of lodging. The launch is the only way to visit the Sunderbans during monsoon.

## Transport

### Digha
**Bus** A/c luxury buses leave from **Kolkata's Esplanade**, taking 4 hrs. Public buses leave from Esplanade and Howrah and take 4½-5 hrs.

**Train** Direct train from Kolkata (H), 5 per day, taking 3-5 hrs.

### Sunderbans Tiger Reserve
It is easiest and most comfortable to visit the reserve on a tour starting from Kolkata, but independent travel is possible and gives you the option of hiring a smaller private boat.

**Bus and boat** From **Kolkata** take **CSTC** bus from Babu Ghat, Strand Rd (1st departure 0630, then hourly until 1330, 3 hrs) to **Sonakhali** (Basanti), from where you can hire a boat to **Sajnekhali** (2½-3 hrs). The alternative (cheaper) option from Basanti is to take an auto to **Gadkhali** (20-30 mins), then a ferry to **Gosaba** (5 mins), then travel across the island by flat-bed van rickshaw (45 mins) to **Pakhiralay** which enables you to see interesting rural life on the way. Finally, take a boat to **Sajnekhali Wildlife Sanctuary** (20 mins) where you will find the **WBTDC Tourist Lodge**.

**Train and boat** From **Kolkata** (S) by (crowded) local train to **Canning** (45 km, 1½ hrs), then a shared auto or bus to **Sonakhali/Basanti** and travel on (as above). From Canning you could get a private boat direct to **Sajnekhali**, but the journey is long (5 hrs) and dependent on the tide.

Motor boat hire with park guide can be arranged at Sajnekhali for around Rs 1200 for 4 hrs, Rs 2000 for 8 hrs; boats can take 6-8 people.

# North
## of Kolkata

Intensely populated and cultivated, the area north of Kolkata has been left wonderfully fertile by both the ever-shifting course of the great Ganga and run-off from the Himalaya. The plains encompass the peaceful university town of Santiniketan, home of Tagore, and the 300-year-old terracotta temples of Bishnupur. The legacy of the Muslim nawabs lives on in the impressive ruins of Gaur and Pandua, while atmospheric Murshidabad provides an accessible blend of Bengali history and relaxation.

## Bishnupur

*terracotta temples and locally made handicrafts*

The warrior Malla Kings of Bengal ruled this area from Bishnupur for nearly two centuries, until the East India Company sold it to the Maharajah of Burdwan in 1805, for arrears of land revenue. The Mallas were great patrons of the arts and built uniquely ornamental terracotta temples. It is also where the Dhrupad style of classical Indian singing originated, as testified by continued existence of the legendary Bishnupur Gharana (School of Music). Local handicrafts include silk, tassar, conch-shell and bell-metalware and the famous terracotta Bankura horse, Dokhra, and also slate statues and artefacts. Bengali sweetmeats and flavoured tobacco are local specialities.

### Sights

There are more than two dozen temples in Bishnupur, mostly dedicated to Krishna and Radha. They are usually built of brick, but sometimes of laterite, and on a square plan with a gently curved roof imitating the Bengali thatched *chala* (hut). The terracotta tiles depict episodes from the *Ramayana* and *Mahabharata*, and also scenes from daily life. Inside, there is a *thakurbari* (sanctuary) and a *vedi* (platform) for the image, on one side. The upper storey has a gallery topped by one, five or even nine towers.

Most of the temples are concentrated within the fort, which was built later by Muslim rulers. Distances given are from the **Tourist Lodge** (see Where to stay). The **Rasmancha** (500 m) is a unique Vishnu shrine with a pyramidal roof, built by Bir Hambir in 1600. It is illuminated at night by coloured floodlights. The well-preserved cannons, in particular the 4-m-long **Dalmadal** to the south of the Rasmancha, date back to the Mallas. Further south is **Jor Mandir** (1 km), a pair of hut-shaped temples with a single *sikhara* flanking a smaller diminutive temple with attractively ornamented panels, built in 1726 by Gopala Singha. The **Shyam Rai Temple** (1 km), perhaps the earliest example of the *pancharatna* (five towers), has a fine *sikhara* and dates from 1643. Each façade is triple arched and the terracotta panels show scenes from the *Ramayana*, the *Mahabharata* and Krishna's life. The large **Madan Mohan Temple** (3 km), with a white façade, was built of brick with terracotta panels in 1694 by King Durjan, while the 17th-century **Lalji** and **Madan Gopal** are built of laterite. The **Mrinmoyee Mandir** (3 km) has a clay idol of Durga dating from AD 997, and in the courtyard a curiosity of nine trees growing together.

Little remains of the Malla kings' **Fort** (2.5 km). You can see the gate of laterite, with firing holes drilled in different directions and a 13th-century stone chariot. The water reservoirs are still there though the moat, once served by seven lakes, is partly dry.

## Essential Bishnupur

### Finding your feet

The town is haphazardly clustered around the Pokabandh Lake; most visitors stay on College Road. Buses from Kolkata and Durgapur drop passengers on the edge of town. The train station is 3 km out of town, from where a cycle-rickshaw to the Tourist Lodge (see Where to stay) costs Rs 30. See Transport, page 68.

### Getting around

It is possible to see all the temples listed on foot (and much more besides), but it's very easy to get lost in the intricate network of streets. Cycle-rickshaws can be hired for Rs 150-200 for two hours.

## Listings Bishnupur

### Where to stay

**$$-$ Tourist Lodge**
*End of College Rd, T03244-252013.*
Lovely clean and spacious rooms, more expensive with a/c, Western toilets, balconies with view over garden, restaurant and bar, breakfast included. Run by WBTDC, it's the best option in town.

### Restaurants

**$ Sree Hotel**
*College Rd, beside Tagore statue.*
*Open 0930-1500, 1800-2000.*
Bengali and South Indian food, excellent *dosas*, great value.

### Festivals

**Aug Jhapan** This regional harvest festival in honour of the serpent goddess Manasa dates from the 17th century. It is linked with the fertility cult and is unique. Venomous snakes (cobras, pythons, vipers, kraits, flying snakes) are brought in baskets by snake-charmers who display amazing tricks.

### Shopping

Cottage industries flourish in the different *paras* (quarters) each devoted to a specialized craft: pottery in Kamarpara, *sankha* (conchshell) cutting in Sankharipara, and weaving, particularly Baluchari silk saris, in Tantipara.

**Silk Khadi Seva Mandal**, Boltala, and **Terracotta Crafts**, 500 m from the Tourist Lodge, are recommended.

**Transport**

**Bus** WBSTC buses to **Kolkata**, 5½ hrs on local roads.

**Train** Trains from **Kolkata** (**H**) to **Bankura**: 5 per day, often running late, 3½-5 hrs.

## Santiniketan

*peaceful rural university, rich in culture and museums*

Santiniketan, the 'Abode of Peace', is a welcome change from the hectic traffic, noise and dirt of Kolkata. Even a brief visit to the shady university campus, with its artistic heritage and its quiet, rural charm, makes a profound impression, and is a must for aficionados of Bengal's greatest poet.

### Vishva Bharati University

*Sightseeing permitted only after university hours: summer 1430-1700, winter 1415-1630 and during holidays 0700-1200; closed Wed and Tue afternoon. No photography. All compounds are subdivided by wire fences.*

The university has an interesting history. The Maharishi Debendranath Tagore, father of Nobel laureate Rabindranath Tagore, started an *ashram* here. In 1901 Rabindranath founded an experimental place of learning with a classroom under the trees, and a group of five pupils. It went on to become the Vishva Bharati University in 1921. It now attracts

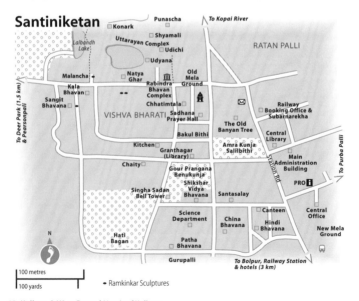

students from all over the world and aspires to be a spiritual meeting ground in a serene, culturally rich and artistic environment. Open-air classes are still a feature of this unique university.

Among the many *Bhavans* are those concentrating on fine art (Kala Bhavan) and music and dance (Sangit Bhavan). The **Uttarayan Complex**, where the poet lived, consists of several buildings in distinctive architectural styles. **Sadhana Prayer Hall**, where Brahmo prayers are held on Wednesday, was founded in 1863. The unusual hall enclosed by stained-glass panels has a polished marble floor which is usually decorated with fresh *alpana* designs. **Chhatimtala**, where Maharishi Debendranath sat and meditated, is the site of special prayers at Convocation time. In keeping with its simplicity, graduates are presented with a twig with five leaves from the locally widespread *Saptaparni* trees.

**Rabindra Bhavan** ① *Uttarayan complex, Thu-Mon 1030-1330 and 1400-1630, Tue 1030-1330; no photography, bags may not be permitted, shoes must be removed before entering each building*. This museum and research centre contains photographs, manuscripts and Tagore's personal belongings; the peripheral buildings also contain photos. The museum is well documented and very informative so allow at least an hour. The garden is delightful, particularly when the roses are blooming.

**Kala Bhavan and Nandan Museum** ① *Thu-Mon 1500-1700*. Kala Bhavan has a rich collection of 20th-century Indian art, particularly sculptures, murals and paintings by famous Bengali artists. **Nandan Museum** ① *Thu-Mon 1000-1330 and 1400-1700, Tue 1000-1330*, has a collection of terracotta, paintings and original tracings of Ajanta murals.

### Around Santiniketan

**Surul** (4 km), with its evocative village atmosphere and small terracotta temples with interesting panels on their façades, makes a pleasant trip. The *zamindari* 'Rajbari' with its durga shrine gives an impression of times past. **Ballavpur Deer Park** (3 km) ① *Thu-Tue 1000-1600*, is a reclaimed wooded area of rapidly eroding laterite *khowai* frequented by spotted deer and winter migratory birds.

## Essential Santiniketan

### Finding your feet

The nearest railway station is Bolpur, which has trains from Kolkata's Haora and Sealdah stations. Cycle-rickshaws charge Rs 30 to Santiniketan, 3 km away. Local buses use a stand near the station. The road journey from Kolkata on the congested NH2 (213 km) can be very slow.

### Getting around

The Vishva Bharati campus and Santiniketan's residential area are ideal for exploring on foot. See Transport, page 70.

## Listings Santiniketan *map p68*

### Tourist information

For general information contact the campus **Public Relations Office (PRO)** (Vishva Bharati Office, T03463-252751, Thu-Tue 1000-1700).

### Where to stay

There are a couple of cheap guesthouses within the campus; to arrange a stay (maximum 3 days) contact the Public Relations Office (PRO; see above).

## $$ Mark and Meadows
*Sriniketan Rd, Birbhum, T03463-264871, www.markandmeadows.com.*
32 cottages in lovely grounds, pool and other activities, and a good multicuisine restaurant. Lively with Bengali families.

## $$-$ Chhuti Holiday Resort
*241 Charupalli, Jamboni, T03463-252692, www.chhutiresort.com.*
Comfortable thatched rooms with bath, some a/c, good restaurant, innovative.

## $$-$ Santiniketan Tourist Lodge (WBTDC)
*Off main road, Bolpur, T03463-252398.*
Slightly faded standard rooms, some quite small, plusher with a/c, pleasant garden, breakfast included (but poor meals).

## $ Manasi Lodge
*Santiniketan Rd, Bolpur, T03463-254200.*
Clean rooms, attached bath, lovely staff, popular courtyard restaurant.

## $ Rangamati
*Prabhat Sarani, Bhubandanga, Bolpur, T03463-252305.*
22 decent rooms, some with balcony, dorm, restaurant (Indian and Chinese).

## $ Royal Bengal
*Bhubandanga, Bolpur, T03463-257148.*
Clean and modern, all rooms with balcony and attached bath, dorm, soulless restaurant.

### Restaurants

## $ Kalor Dokan
*Open all hours.*
An institution since the time of Tagore.

## $ Maduram
*Santiniketan Rd, Bolpur.*
Highly recommended sweet shop.

### Fact...
Bauls are Bengal's wandering minstrels, who are worshippers of Vishnu. They travel from village to village singing their songs, accompanied by a single string instrument, *ektara*, and a tiny drum.

### Festivals

Programmes of dance, music and singing are held throughout the year, but are particularly good during festivals.

**End Jan/early Feb** **Magh Mela**, an agricultural and rural crafts fair at Sriniketan marks the anniversary of the founding of Brahmo Samaj. **Vasanta Utsav** coincides with **Holi**.
**Late Dec** (check with Bengal TIC) **Poush Mela**, an important fair, coinciding with the village's **Foundation Day**. Folk performances include Santals dances and Baul songs.

### Shopping

The local embossed leather work is distinctive.

**Smaranika Handicraft Centre**, *opposite Bolpur Station*. Sells interesting embroidery, jewellery and saris at fixed prices.
**Subarnarekha**, *next to railway booking office in Santiniketan*. Sells rare books.
**Suprabhat Women Handicrafts**, *Prabhat Sarani, Bhuban Nagar, opposite Tourist Lodge, Bolpur, open 0930-1300, 1700-1900*. Excellent, creative embroidery (including *kantha*), ready made or to order, crafted by local women.

### Transport

**Train** Many trains from **Kolkata** (**H**) to Bolpur, near Santiniketan, taking 2½-3½ hrs. Also trains to NJP (for **Darjeeling**) via **Malda**.

**historic mosques, palaces and ruins set on a beautiful stretch of river**

Named after Nawab Murshid Kuli Khan, a Diwan under Emperor Aurangzeb, Murshidabad became the capital of Bengal in 1705 and remained so until the battle of Plassey. The town lies on the east bank of the Bhagirathi, a picturesque tributary of the Ganga, with imposing ruins scattered around and an enchanting time-warp feel. A vibrant vegetable bazar takes place each morning beneath decaying columns left over from the days of the nawabs, and the town comes to life for the famed Muslim festival of Muhurram at the end of January. Woven and handblock-printed silk saris and bell-metal ware are the main local industries. Come during the week to avoid the crowds.

## Nizamat Kila

Located on the river bank, Nizamat Kila was the site of the old fort and encloses the nawabs' Italianate **Hazarduari** ('1000 doors') **Palace** ① *Sat-Thu 1000-1500, Rs 100, no photography*, built in 1837. It is now a splendid museum with a portrait gallery, library and circular durbar hall and contains a rare collection of old arms, curios, china and paintings. The large newer **Imambara** (1847) opposite, also Italianate in style, is under a continuous process of renovation and is worth exploring. The domed, square **Madina** (pavillion) with a veranda that stands nearby may be what remains of the original Imambara.

## Other sights

There are numerous 18th-century monuments in the town which are best visited by cycle-rickshaw (Rs 200-300 for three hours). Mir Jafar and his son Miran lived at **Jafaragunj Deorhi**, known as the traitor's gate. **Kat-gola** ① *Rs 50*, the atmospheric garden palace of a rich Jain merchant, houses a collection of curios including Belgian glass mirror-balls and has an old Jain temple and boating 'lake' in the grounds. The **Palace of Jagat Sett**, one of the richest financiers of the 18th century, is 2 km from the Jafargung cemetery to the north of the palace. The brick ruins of **Katra Masjid** (1723), modelled on the great mosque at Mecca and an important centre of learning, are outside the city to the east. It was built by Murshid Kuli Khan who lies buried under the staircase. **Moti Jheel** (Pearl Lake) and the ruins of **Begum Ghaseti's Palace** are 2 km south of the city; only a mosque and a room remain. **Khosbagh** (Garden of Delight), across the river and easily accessible by bamboo ferries (Rs 1), has three walled enclosures.

> **Tip...**
> Hire a boat (through **Hotel Manjusha**) and journey upstream to Baranagar to see three well-preserved terracotta temples in the Bangla style. Drift back down, stopping off at the Jain town of Azimganj on the way.

### Where to stay

$ Ashoke Mahal
*Omrahaganj, T03482-320855.*
Clean and pleasant, rear room 202 is the best with a balcony overlooking the river.

$ Indrajit
*Near railway station, T03482-271858,*
*http://hotelindrajit.in.*
Wide choice of rooms of all standards, some a/c, friendly staff. Truly excellent multi-cuisine restaurant; the Indian dishes are especially recommended, serves strong beer.

$ Manjusha
*By Hazarduari Palace, T03482-270321.*
The best location in town, with serene riverside setting for spotting dolphins, lush garden of flowers and fruit trees, charming manager can help with bike, rickshaw and boat hire. Rooms are simple with fans. Food isn't recommended.

$ Sagnik
*77 Omrahaganj, T03482-271492,*
*www.hotelsagnik.com.*
Newer hotel with some a/c rooms, check a few, some allow glimpses of the river. Tiny tiled bathrooms, TVs and keen staff.

### Festivals

Late Dec (check with Bengal TIC) **Muharram**, a fair lasting a few days, which culminates in a 6-hr procession through the village.

### Transport

**Bus** Buses between Berhampur and Kolkata are painful.

**Train** Many trains daily to **Berhampur** (for Murshidabad) direct *Lalgola Passenger 53181* from **Kolkata (S)** leaves 2345, 5 hrs, daily; also *Sealdah Lalgola Pass 53173* at 0800. From Murshidabad, the *Bagirathi Mail 13104*, 0615, taking 4 hrs back to Sealdah is best. Arriving from northern destinations, trains stop at New Farakka from where it's a 2-bus to **Berhampur**. Jeeps/shared autos run from Berhampur local bus stand to **Lalbagh** near Murshidabad, 30-40 mins. Then catch a cycle-rickshaw to Hazarduari gate, Rs 30.

## Gaur, Pandua and Malda
### ruins of medieval Islamic capitals, off the beaten path

Gaur's situation on the banks of the River Ganga, yet within easy reach of the Rajmahal Hills with their fine black basalt, made it possible for gifted stonemasons to construct beautiful religious and secular buildings. Muslim monuments of the sultanate period are strewn around the quiet, deserted city. Pandua alternated with Gaur as a capital of Bengal between 1338 and 1500, when it was abandoned. Some of the ruins here show clearly how the Muslims made free use of material from Hindu temples near Malda.

### Malda
Malda is a convenient and comfortable base from which to visit the atmospheric ruins of Gaur and Pandua, with plenty of banks and other amenities in the town centre. Now famous mainly for its large juicy Fajli mangoes, Malda was established around 1680 by the English, who bought an entire village from a local landlord and expanded it into a market town.

Malda has some worthy sights of its own, including the **Malda Museum** (1937), which has a collection of stone images, coins and inscriptions from Gaur and Pandua. The **market** behind the **Tourist Lodge** is fascinating. Old Malda, which lies at a confluence of rivers 4 km away, is the site of the **Jami Masjid**, built in 1596 out of decorated brick and stone with some good carving on the entrance pillars. The 17-m **Nimasarai Tower** across the river dates from the same period, and has strange stones embedded on the outer surface, which may once have been used to display beheaded criminals.

## Gaur

*Most visitors arrange a half-day taxi tour of the sites, through the tourist office in Malda. But getting to the sites on local transport has its own rewards: take a bus for Mohodipur from near the Tourist Lodge in Malda, and ask to be dropped at Pyasbari (tea and snacks available). Stay on the narrow tarmac road and you won't get lost. Turn right from the NH34 for the site, which you can wander around for free. To return to Malda, stop a bus or share a taxi.*

On the ancient site of Lakshanavati, Gaur was the capital of King Sasanka in the seventh century, followed by the Buddhist Pala kings. The city became famous as a centre of education and culture during the reign of the Hindu Sena kings in the 12th century. In the early 13th century it was invaded by Bhaktiar Khalji and then captured by the Afghan Fakhr-ud-din Dynasty in the 14th century. They plundered the temples to construct their own mosques and tombs. During the 15th century, a number of mosques and mausoleums were built in the new architectural style. Gaur was sacked by Sher Shah Suri in 1537 and the city's population was wiped out by plague in 1575.

The great golden mosque, **Bari Sona Masjid** or Baroduari (12-door), was built in 1526 and is an enormous rectangular stone-faced brick structure with a large open square in front. Fine marble carving is still visible on the remains of the minarets. Note the small Kali temple at the entrance.

**Ramkeli**, not far from the Bari Sona Masjid, has the Madan Mohan Jiu Mandir and is of religious significance for followers of **Sri Chaitanya**, the 14th-century Bengali religious reformer. **Tamaltola** marks where he meditated under a tree. Pilgrims come to see a footprint in stone.

The remains of the embankments of Gaur fort are to the south on the bank of the Bhagirati. Bangladesh can be seen from the **Dakhil Darwaza** (early 15th century), the main fort gateway with its five-storeyed towers. It was built of small red bricks embossed with terracotta decorations. The turrets and circular bastions produce a striking contrast of light and shade with decorative motifs of suns, rosettes, lamps and fretted borders. The **Firuz Minar** (Victory Tower), built by Sultan Firuz Shah in 1486, has a spiral staircase. The lower storeys are 12 sided while the upper are circular, with striking blue and white glazed tiles, used in addition to the terracotta and brick.

The builders of the **Chika Mosque** ('Bat Mosque', early 15th century), near the Kadam Rasul, made free use of Hindu idols in its construction. The **Chamkati Mosque** (circa 1475) shows the vaulted ceiling of the veranda. Inside the southeast corner of the fort is the massive **Baisgazi Wall**, which enclosed the old palace with its *darbar,* harem, etc.

**Kadam Rasul** (1513) is a domed building with a Bengali *chala* roof, which housed the relic of the Prophet, a footprint in stone. The two-storeyed **Lukochuri Darwaza** (Hide-and-Seek Gate, circa 1655) is in the later Mughal style.

The **Tantipara Mosque** (circa 1475; *tanti*, weaver) has superbly decorated red brick with octagonal turrets and five entrance arches. The elegant **Lattan (Painted) Mosque** (1475), attributed to Yusuf Shah, was decorated with bands of blue, green, yellow and white glazed tiles. Some 2 km south, close to the Bangladeshi border, the ruined **Chhoti Sona Masjid** has a carved gate.

## Pandua

*To get to the site by public transport, take a Siliguri or Raiganj bus from the Tourist Lodge in Malda and ask to be dropped at Pandua bus stand. The old brick-paved road, nearly 4 m wide and about 10 km long, passes through the village giving a fascinating behind-the-scenes view of Bengali life, and most of the monuments lie close to it. Buses from Adina return to Malda.*

The **Adina Masjid** (1364-1374) exemplifies Muslim architecture in medieval Bengal. Built by Sultan Sikander Shah and once comparable to the great eighth-century mosque at Damascus, it is sadly in a poor state of repair. The vast space enclosed by pillared aisles has an 88-arch screen around a quadrangle with the mosque. Influence of 12th-century Sena architecture is evident in the tall, ornate, tiered *sikhara* and trefoil arches and the remarkable absence of a large entrance gateway. Most of the substructure and some pillars were of basalt plundered from existing Hindu temples and palaces. A small doorway in the western back wall of the mosque, clearly taken from an earlier Vishnu temple, exhibits the stonemasons' skill and the exceptional metalwork of the time.

The **Eklakhi Mausoleum**, built of brick (circa 1412), has a Hindu idol carved on its front lintel. The **Qutb Shahi Mosque** (also *Sona* or Golden Mosque) was built in 1582. Further along are the ruins of the 17th-century **Chhoti** and **Bari Dargahs**.

## Listings Gaur, Pandua and Malda

## Where to stay

### Malda

**$ Continental Lodge**
*22 KJ Sanyal Rd, by State Bus Stand, T03512-252388, www.continentallodge.com.*
Reasonable range of rooms, restaurant, friendly, views over town from public balcony.

**$ Tourist Lodge**
*NH34, T03512-220911.*
13 rooms around courtyard, some a/c, bar, restaurant.

## Transport

### Malda

**Road** Buses, taxis and *tongas* are available for trips to **Gaur** and **Pandua**, Bus to **Murshidabad**, 3-4 hrs. **Siliguri**, WBSTC Rocket buses 1700-2400, 6½ hrs. Bus to Kolkata not recommended.

**Train** To **NJP**: for Darjeeling, several trains daily, around 4½ hrs. **Kolkata (S)**: *Kanchenjunga Exp 15658*, 1235, 7 hrs.

# West
## Bengal Hills

The Himalayan foothills of northern West Bengal contain a wealth of trekking opportunities and hill stations in stunning locations, including the region's prime tourist destination, Darjeeling. The old colonial summer retreat is surrounded by spectacular views and still draws plenty of visitors to enjoy cooler climes and a good cuppa. The smaller, less touristed hill stations of Kalimpong, Kurseong and Mirik also offer wonderful walking and a relaxed vibe. The area also holds one of the Indian one-horned rhino's last safe havens in the Jaldapara Wildlife Sanctuary.

## Siliguri and around

gateway to the hills and wildlife parks

### Siliguri

Surrounded by tea plantations, Siliguri is a largely unattractive transport hub with busy main roads lined with shops, a couple of good markets and one of the largest stupas in India (30 m) at **Salugara Monastery**, 5 km away. The town is a stopping-off point for travel into the hills and to some national parks in the vicinity. Visitors spend a night here if they wish to ride the Darjeeling Himalayan Railway (DHR), which has UNESCO World Heritage listing (see box, page 84).

### Jaldapara Wildlife Sanctuary

*T0353-2511974, www.jaldapara.in. Public access 16 Sep-14 Jun only, Rs 150, still camera Rs 50. Elephant safari daily 0600-0800, Rs 750 per person for 1 hr. Guide fees Rs 1600 for 6 people.*

The River Torsa flows through Jaldapara Wildlife Sanctuary, which covers an area of 216 sq km (only 30 sq km is open to tourists) and is situated close to Phuntsholing in Bhutan. The riverine forests of sal, khair and sheeshu harbour the one-horned rhino, elephants, leopards, gaur (Indian bison), wild boar, several species of deer and sloth bears. Ornithologists come to see crested and fishing eagles, and the rare Bengal florican. Elephant and jeep safaris are available to take visitors around, and there is good accommodation in the form of tourist lodges which are bookable in Siliguri. The best time to visit is from October to April, when forest cover is thinner and animals are easier to spot.

# BACKGROUND

## West Bengal

In prehistoric times Bengal was home to Dravidian hunter-gatherers. In the first millennium BC, the Aryans from Central Asia, who had learned agricultural techniques and the art of weaving and pottery, arrived in Bengal, bringing with them the Sanskrit language. From about the fifth century BC trade in cotton, silk and coral from Ganga Nagar flourished. In the third century BC, Bengal was part of the Mauryan Empire.

The Guptas conquered Bengal in the fourth century AD and trade with the Mediterranean expanded for the next 200 years, particularly with Rome. The fall of the Roman Empire in the fifth century led to a decline in Bengal's fortunes. Only with the founding of the Pala Dynasty in AD 750 was the region united once again. Bengal became a centre of Buddhism, and art and learning flourished. The Senas followed. They were great patrons of the arts and ruled for 50 years until deposed by the invading Turks, who began a century of Muslim rule under the Khaljis of the Delhi Sultanate. The most notable of the Pathan kings who followed the Khaljis was Sher Shah, who extended his territory from Bihar into Bengal. The land was taken back by the Mughal emperor Akbar in 1574-1576, who wanted the rich resources of rice, silk and saltpetre.

The increasing power of the Muslims lured the Portuguese towards the subcontinent, and they began trading with Bengal in the mid-16th century. Before long they faced competition from the Dutch and the British, and in 1632 an attack on their port near Kolkata by Emperor Shah Jahan reduced their merchant power.

In 1690 the purchase of the three villages which grew into Calcutta enabled the British to build a fort and consolidate their power. In 1700, Bengal became an

About a 1000-strong population of the Toto tribe still maintain their traditions and customs in the village of **Totopara**, 30 km to the north of the sanctuary.

### Gorumara National Park

*90 km east of Siliguri, www.dooarstourism.com. Public access 16 Sep-14 Jun only; closed Thu. Rs 70-120 (depending which watchtower you visit), still camera free, video Rs 200, jeep Rs 700-1200 for up to 6 persons, guide Rs 150.*

Located in the Dooars (meaning 'door' in Bengali and Assamese) region, the Gorumara National Park is an interesting diversion little visited by foreign tourists. Covering 85 sq km, the riverine grasslands and forests hide rhinos, gaur, leopard, elephants, deer and more than 200 species of bird. A few watchtowers give great views and the chance to spot elephants as they come to water.

independent presidency and Calcutta prospered. The *firmans* (permits) granted were for trading from the ports but the British gained a monopoly over internal trade as well. After the death of Emperor Aurangzeb, the authority of Delhi slowly crumbled. In 1756, Siraj-ud-Daula, the then Nawab of Bengal, noticed Kolkata's growing wealth. He attacked Fort William and captured the city. Within a year, however, Clive took the city back and then defeated the Nawab at Plassey; a turning point for the British in India.

During the 19th century West Bengal became the economic and political centre of British India, and Calcutta developed as the principal centre of cultural and political activity. Bengali literature, drama, art and music flourished. Religious reform movements such as the Brahmo Samaj, under the leadership of Raja Ra Mohan Roy in the 1830s, developed from the juxtaposition of traditional Hinduism with Christian missionary activity at the beginning of the 19th century. Later, one of India's greatest poets, Nobel Prize winner Rabindranath Tagore (1861-1941), dominated India's cultural world, breathing moral and spiritual life into the political movement for independence.

Until 1905 Bengal had included much of modern Bihar and Orissa, as well as the whole of Bengal. Lord Curzon's short-lived Partition of Bengal in 1905 roused fierce opposition and also encouraged the split between Muslims and Hindus which finally resulted in Bengali Muslim support for the creation of Pakistan in 1947. The division into the two new states was accompanied by the migration of over five million people and appalling massacres as Hindus and Muslims fled. West Bengal was again directly affected by the struggle to create Bangladesh, when about 10 million refugees arrived from East Pakistan after 25 March 1971. Most returned after Bangladesh gained its Independence in December 1971.

## Listings Siliguri and around

### Tourist information

GTA (Gorkhaland Territorial Administration)
*Opposite WBTDC, Hill Cart Rd, T0353-251 1974/9, www.gtatourism.com. Mon-Fri 0900-1700, Sat-Sun 0900-1300.*
This tourism office takes bookings for its lodges in North Bengal.

WBTDC
*1st floor, 4 Hill Cart Rd, T0353-251 7561. Mon-Fri 1000-1730, also at NJP Station and airport.*
Provides useful information. The Forest Development Corporation in the main office books the lodges in Jaldapara Wildlife Sanctuary.

### Where to stay

**Siliguri**
Hill Cart Rd is officially Tenzing Norgay Rd.

**$$$ Cindrella**
*Sevoke Rd, '3rd mile' (out of town), T0353-254 7136, www.cindrellahotels.com.*
Comfortable a/c rooms, pool, competent vegetarian restaurant, internet, car hire, pick-up from airport, breakfast included. Drinks in the bar or on the rather lovely roof terrace are a drawcard.

**$$-$ Conclave**
*Hill Cart Rd, T0353-251 6144.*
Good-quality rooms, a/c, satellite TV, licensed bar, **Eminent** restaurant serving Indian/European food, internet, parking.

### $$-$ Vinayak
*Hill Cart Rd, T0353-243 1130,*
*www.vinayakonline.com.*
Clean rooms with bath, some a/c, good
restaurant, look at a few rooms, some of
the budget options are better than others.

### $ Anjali Lodge
*Nabin Sen Rd (next to the Gurudwara),*
*off Sevoke Rd, T0353-252 2964.*
Institutional building, bright white paint
throughout, large rooms with concrete
floors have clean sheets, towels, soap, TV,
cheaper without a/c, some have balcony or
there is spacious public balcony. Suspicious
staff soon warm up.

### $ Mainak Tourist Lodge (WBTDC)
*Hill Cart Rd (opposite main bus stand),*
*T0353-251 2859, www.wbtdc.gov.in.*
Large and open 1970s-style hotel,
comfortable rooms (check a few, they vary),
14 a/c, and some $$ suites. Set back from
the road in dusty gardens, with restaurant
and bar, helpful staff. Be sure not to overlap
with a wedding party; call ahead.

### $ Siliguri Lodge
*Hill Cart Rd (near SNT bus stand),*
*T0353-251 5290.*
A rock-bottom basic option, grotty exterior
but clean sheets and relatively quiet, being
set back from the road. Kind staff.

## Jaldapara Wildlife Sanctuary

### $$ Hollong Forest Tourist Lodge
*Hollong, 6 km from Madarihat, T03563-*
*262228, book well in advance (4 months)*
*either directly, online at www.wbtdc.gov.in, or*
*via the Tourist Bureau, Siliguri, T0353-251 1974.*
Built of timber, on stilts, deep inside
the sanctuary. 6 rooms, excellent meals,
the lodge is very popular.

## Gorumara National Park

### $$$ Riverwood Forest Retreat
*www.waxpolhotels.com.*
This eco-friendly resort has lush surrounds,
and some balconies have views of mountain
peaks. Comfortable well-appointed rooms,
fitness centre, library, pool, and plenty of
other activities. Guided excursions into
Gorumara, plus day treks, village visits
and tea tourism.

## Restaurants

### Siliguri

### $$ Havelli
*SS Market Complex, Hill Cart Rd,*
*T(0)9800803395. Open 1100-2230.*
Subtly lit, beige walls and wood sculptures
prevail, more intimate than most.
Multicuisine is high standard and the
choices endless. Family atmosphere.

### $$-$ Khana Khazana
*Hill Cart Rd. Open 0700-2230.*
Pleasant outdoor terrace plus indoor seating
(fans), generous portions, South Indian is
decent or there's a choice of tandoori, rolls,
Chinese, veg/non-veg, but *lassis* and shakes
are average. Clean family atmosphere.

### $$-$ Rasoi
*Ganeshayan Building (2nd floor),*
*beside Sky Star Building, Sevoke Rd,*
*T(0)99758-802071. Open 1030-2230.*
Pure veg food in a modern spacious
environment, great for kebabs and South
Indian (40 kinds of *dosa*), interesting *dhals*,
plus some Chinese options.

### $ Amit's Amardeep
*7 Sevoke Rd. Open 0830-2230.*
Upstairs a/c, cheap youthful place with
North Indian and Chinese, good biryani,
friendly able staff.

## BORDER CROSSING
### To Nepal

#### Panitanki–Kakarbhitta (Kakarvita)
Jeeps go frequently from Siliguri, as well as from Darjeeling, to Panitanki on the east bank of a wide river that forms the border here between India and Nepal. A small notice and an Indian flag are all that mark the Indian immigration checkpost, which is in a shady grove of trees by the road.

Kakarbhitta (Kakarvita) is on the Nepalese side, linked by a kilometre-long road bridge. Cycle rickshaws run between the two towns. Kakarbhitta has only basic accommodation. Single or multiple-entry 30-day visas for Nepal cost US$40, to be paid in cash (15-day US$25, 90-day US$100).

From the border, buses depart 0300-2400, arriving in Kathmandu (595 km) 16-17 hours later; the journey can be very tiring. It is also possible to fly (seasonally) from Bhadrapur (24 km from Kakarbhitta) to Kathmandu with Buddha Air or Yeti Airlines (50 minutes). Alternatively, get a taxi to Biratnagar in Nepal (150 km) and fly from there to Kathmandu.

**$ Jain Jaika Bhojnalaya**
*Shikha Deep Building (3rd floor), Sevoke Rd.*
*Opens 0800-1530, 1830-2130.*
Look for their red-and-white sign down a tiny alley (there's a lift). Sunny orange walls and a chequered floor, pure veg food, best as a breakfast option (excellent *paratha* and veg – other items on menu generally unavailable).

### What to do

#### Siliguri
**Tour operators**
**Help Tourism (Association of Conservation & Tourism)**, *143 Hill Cart Rd, 1st floor, T0353-253 5893, www.helptourism. com*. Recommended for eastern Himalaya and arranging homestays in villages around the tea gardens.

### Transport

#### Siliguri
**Air** Bagdogra Airport, 13 km away, has daily flights to **Kolkata**, **Guwahati**, **Delhi** and **Chennai**. Pawan Hans helicopter goes twice daily in fine weather to/from **Gangtok**,

T03592-203960, 35 mins, Rs 3500, maximum luggage weight strictly 10 kg. Taxis from airport to Darjeeling, Gangtok, Kalimpong, Siliguri and NJP charge set rates.

**Bus** Tenzing Norgay Central Bus Terminus (CBT) is on Hill Cart Rd, next to Siliguri Junction Railway Station. There are also many private operators just outside the CBT offering similar services. To **Madarihat** (for Jaldapara) leaves from the CBT at 0700, 3 hrs; to **Malda**, frequent buses from 0430-2300, 6 hrs. The WBSTC's overnight Rocket bus to **Kolkata** departs 1800, 1900 and 2000 from Hill Cart Rd, 12 hrs, but it's a tortuous journey on terrible roads. For greater comfort on a Volvo bus try **Gupta Tour & Travels**, T0353-645 4077, departing at 2000. Ticket counter 13 in the CBT for buses to Assam: **Guwahati** at 1700, 12 hrs; **Tezpur** at 1400, 16 hrs. **SNT Bus Station**, is opposite CBT: **Gangtok**, buses leave regularly between 0730-1330, 5 hrs; deluxe private buses from CBT (separate ticket window).

**To Bhutan** Bhutan Government buses, tickets from Counter 14 at CBT, 0700-1200. To **Phuntsholing**: buses at 0720, 1200,

1400, 1500, 3-4 hrs. **NBSTC** buses run at 0700 and 1200.

**To Nepal** To **Kathmandu** buses (or more conveniently taxi or jeep, every 15 mins or so from opposite CBT) to **Panitanki** on the border (35 km, 1 hr); transfer to **Kakarbhitta** by cycle-rickshaw. Through tickets are available from private bus companies.

**Jeep** Kalimpong (54 km), from Sevoke Rd stand, 2½ hrs; **Gangtok** (114 km), Sevoke Rd or outside CBT on Hill Cart Rd, 3½-4 hrs; **Darjeeling** (80 km), from Hill Cart Rd, 3 hrs; **Kurseong**, from Hill Cart Rd (near Conclave Hotel), 1½ hrs; **Mirik**, from Hill Cart Rd, opposite CBT, 2 hrs; and from the same place to **Jorethang**, 3½ hrs (you need to have an ILP in advance to cross this border). Jeeps also leave from outside NJP direct for Darjeeling, Kalimpong and Gangtok, at a slightly higher price and with some waiting while drivers tout for customers.

**Train** Siliguri is served by 2 railway stations: **Siliguri Junction** and **NJP**, 5 km away; both have tourist information. There are buses, *tempos* (Rs 15), cycle-rickshaws (Rs 60) and taxis (Rs 150) between the 2. Note that rickshaw drivers can be quite aggressive

at NJP. NJP has good connections to other major destinations in India. Several daily from NJP to **Kolkata,** best is the *Darjeeling Mail 12344*, 2000, 10 hrs, finishing at Sealdah. To **Delhi**: at least 5 trains per day, best is the *Rajdhani Exp 12423*, 1315, 21 hrs. Try to arrive at Siliguri or NJP in daylight (before 1900).

To **Darjeeling** (via **Kurseong**) the *Toy Train* leaves from NJP, calling at Siliguri Junction on its way. The daily diesel service leaves at 0900, 7½ hrs, though in reality the journey is usually 9 hrs, and services are often disrupted by landslides during the monsoon. In high season, a **Toy Train Jungle Safari** runs at 1000 to Tindharia village, a 6-hr round journey, Rs 595, going through Mahanada Wildlife Sanctuary. These trips are bookable at Siliguri Junction or on the **IRCTC** website www.irctc.co.in.

Jaldapara
**Bus** Buses from **Siliguri** to **Madarihat**, then change for Jaldapara Park. There is Forest Department transport to Hollong inside the sanctuary.

**Train** Hasimara station (18 km from park) has several trains daily to **Siliguri Junction** including: *Mahananda Exp 14083*, 0752, 2½ hrs.

## Darjeeling and around

**mountain views, tea gardens and a holiday vibe**

For tens of thousands of visitors from Kolkata and the steamy plains, Darjeeling is a place to escape the summer heat. Built on a crescent-shaped ridge, the town is surrounded by hills that are thickly covered with coniferous forests and terraced tea gardens. The idyllic setting, the exhilarating air outside town, and stunning views of the Kangchenjunga range (when you can see through the clouds) attract plenty of trekkers too. However, modern reality means that Darjeeling's lower market area resembles any other crowded, noisy, polluted Indian town.

## Sights

The **Mahakal Mandir** atop **Observatory Hill**, sacred to Siva, is a pleasant walk, but the views of the mountains are obscured by tall trees. Sacred to both Hindus and Buddhists, the temple is active and colourful, with prayer flags tied to every tree and pole in the

# Essential Darjeeling

## Finding your feet

**Bagdogra**, near Siliguri, is Darjeeling's nearest airport. The narrow-gauge diesel 'toy train' runs from Siliguri/NJP at 0900 in season and is picturesque but very slow, supposedly taking seven hours, but in reality taking much longer (see box, page 84). Most people reach Darjeeling by jeep and arrive at the motor stand in the lower town, though some go to **Clubside** on The Mall, which is more convenient for most accommodation. In the pedestrianized centre of town, on the ridge, **Chowrasta** is the natural heart of Darjeeling and particularly atmospheric at dawn and dusk.

## Getting around

Most of Darjeeling's roads slope quite gently so it is easy to walk around the town. The lower and upper roads are linked by a series of connecting roads and steep steps. For

### Tip...

Tensions sometimes flare in the region over demands for a separate Gorkha (ethnic Nepali) state to be carved out of West Bengal. Protests result in strikes (*bandhs*), road closures and occasional violence, although this is never directed at foreigners.

sights away from the centre you need to hire a taxi; these are readily available in the lower part of town.

## When to go

Between June and September the monsoons bring heavy downpours, sometimes causing landslides, but the air clears after mid-September. Winter evenings are cold enough to demand log fires and lots of warm clothing. Be prepared for seasonal water shortages and frequent power cuts. After dark a torch is essential.

---

vicinity. Beware of the monkeys as they bite. Further along Jawahar Road West is **Shrubbery (Nightingale) Park**, a pleasant detour if it's still too early to visit the zoo. Views to the north are excellent from the renovated park, and evening cultural shows take place here (information from the GTA tourist office).

**Padmaja Naidu Himalayan Zoological Park** ⓘ *www.pnhzp.gov.in. Daily 0830-1630 (summer), 0830-1600 (winter) except Thu, Rs 100.* The zoo houses high-altitude wildlife including Himalayan black bears, Siberian tigers, Tibetan wolves and plenty of red pandas, as well as deer, a multitude of birds and the gorgeously marked rare clouded leopard. There are large enclosures over a section of the hillside, though at feeding time and during wet weather the animals retreat into their small cement enclosures giving the impression that they are restricted to their cells. The zoo has a reasonably successful snow leopard breeding programme, with over 40 births since 1983, and is the only Asian zoo to have successfully introduced red pandas into the wild.

**Himalayan Mountaineering Institute** ⓘ *Entrance through the zoo on Jawahar Rd West, T0354-227 0158, no photography, entrance fee included in zoo ticket.* Previously headed by Tenzing Norgay, who shared the first successful climb of Everest in 1953, the Institute runs training courses during dry months of the year (see page 90). Within the complex, the

**Everest Museum** traces the history of attempted climbs from 1857, and the **Mountaineering Museum** displays old equipment including that used on the historic Tenzing-Hillary climb.

**Darjeeling Ropeway** ⓘ *Lebong Cart Rd, Singamari, open daily, summer 1000-1400, winter 1000-1600, Rs 150.* Starting from Singamari, the cable car offers magnificent views over the

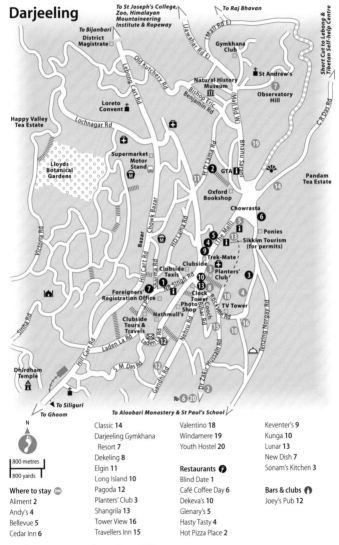

# Darjeeling

**Where to stay**
Aliment **2**
Andy's **4**
Bellevue **5**
Cedar Inn **6**
Classic **14**
Darjeeling Gymkhana
 Resort **7**
Dekeling **8**
Elgin **11**
Long Island **10**
Pagoda **12**
Planters' Club **3**
Shangrila **13**
Tower View **16**
Travellers Inn **15**
Valentino **18**
Windamere **19**
Youth Hostel **20**

**Restaurants** 🍴
Blind Date **1**
Café Coffee Day **6**
Dekeva's **10**
Glenary's **5**
Hasty Tasty **4**
Hot Pizza Place **2**
Keventer's **9**
Kunga **10**
Lunar **13**
New Dish **7**
Sonam's Kitchen **3**

**Bars & clubs** 🎷
Joey's Pub **12**

Darjeeling means region of the *dorje* (thunderbolt) and its official but rarely used spelling is Darjiling. The surrounding area once belonged to Sikkim, although parts were annexed from time to time by the Bhutanese and Nepalese. The East India Company returned the territory's sovereignty to the Rajas of Sikkim, which led to the British obtaining permission to gain the site of the hill station called Darjeeling in 1835, in return for an annual payment. It was practically uninhabited and thickly forested but soon grew into a popular health resort after a road and several houses were built and tea growing was introduced. The Bengal government escaped from the Kolkata heat to take up its official summer residence here. The upper reaches were originally occupied by the Europeans, who built houses with commanding views. Down the hillside on terraces sprawled the humbler huts and bazars of the Indian town.

Rangeet Valley during the 15-minute ride down to Tukva. Note that in high season, there can be queues for over an hour to board.

**Natural History Museum** ① *Bishop Eric Benjamin Rd, daily 0900-1630, Rs 10.* The decaying Natural History Museum was set up in 1903 and has a large collection of fauna of the region and a certain charm; the basement has a curious diorama and specimen jars.

**Tibetan Refugee Self-help Centre** ① *North of town (from Chowrasta, take the lane to the right towards the viewpoint, and then walk down for about 30 mins and ask), www.tibetancentredarjeeling.com. Mon-Sat 0800-1700, closes for lunch.* After the Chinese invasion, thousands of Tibetan refugees settled in Darjeeling (many having accompanied the Dalai Lama) and the rehabilitation centre, with its temple, school and hospital, was set up in 1959 to enable them to continue to practise their skills and provide a sales outlet. You can watch carpet weaving, spinning, dyeing, woodwork, etc, during the season, when the centre is well worth a visit. The shop sells fabulous woollen carpets (orders taken and posted), textiles, curios and jewellery, though these are not cheap to buy.

On the way to the refugee centre is the lovely **Bhutia Bustee Monastery**, which was built on Observatory Hill in 1765 but was moved to its present position in 1861. Someone will show you around and point out gold-flecked murals that have been gorgeously restored.

**Lloyd Botanical Gardens** ① *Near the market, Mon-Sat 0600-1700.* These were laid out in 1878 on land given by Mr W Lloyd, owner of the Lloyd's Bank. They have a modest collection of Himalayan and Alpine flora, including banks of azaleas and rhododendrons, magnolias, a good hothouse (with over 50 species of orchid) and a herbarium. It is a pleasant and quiet spot. **Victoria Falls**, which is only impressive in the monsoons, provides added interest to a three-hour nature trail.

**Aloobari Monastery** South of town, the Aloobari Monastery, on Tenzing Norgay Road, is open to visitors. Tibetan and Sikkimese handicrafts made by the monks are for sale.

## ON THE ROAD

## Darjeeling Himalayan Railway – a mini miracle

Travelling on the somewhat erratic narrow-gauge 'Toy Train' between New Jalpaiguri (NJP) and Darjeeling, which used to be hauled by sparkling tank engines, is a rewarding experience. The brainchild of East Bengal Railway agent Franklyn Prestage, the railway line improved access to the hills from the sweltering humidity of the Kolkata plains in the summer and was completed in 1881. It is a stunning achievement, winding its way up the hillside, often with brilliant views over the plains, covering the 82 km with gradients of up to 1:19. At Ghoom it reaches 2438 m and then descends 305 m to Darjeeling. The service was suspended for five years recently, due to a landslide, but reopened in June 2015. (For details of the tourist steam service between Darjeeling and Ghoom, see page 84).

**Lebong Race Course** The disused Lebong Race Course, 8 km from Darjeeling, was once the smallest and highest in the world and makes a pleasant walk, heading down from Chowrasta. It was started as a parade ground in 1885, and there is now talk of it becoming a race course once more.

### Darjeeling to Ghoom (Ghum)

It is highly recommended to make the 11-km (45-minute) journey to Ghoom from Darjeeling by **steam train**, ending up at the highest railway station in India (also see box, above). All trains pass through **Batasia Loop**, 5 km from Darjeeling, where the narrow-gauge rail does a figure-of-eight loop. There's a war memorial here in a pleasant park with good mountain views. A few spruced-up carriages offer a tourist-only ride in summer with a photo stop at **Batasia**; bookings must be made 90 days in advance, although it is possible to buy spare seats on the day from agents who have private counters set up at Darjeeling station. Three steam trains make the return journey at 1040, 1310 and 1605, Rs 1090; a diesel train runs at 0800, Rs 625 (all seats are first class). A much more economical option is to take the passenger steam train at 1015, which goes to Kurseong (first class Rs 210; second class Rs 60) via Ghoom (Rs 140/30). From Ghoom, you can also return to Darjeeling on foot or by jeep.

**Sights in Ghoom (Ghum)** The little **Railway Museum** ⓘ *daily 1000-1300 and 1400-1600, Rs 20, buy your ticket from the station and staff will unlock the gate,* outlines the history of the Darjeeling Himalayan Railway and has some interesting old photos. Also at **Ghoom** is the important **Yiga Choeling Gompa**, a Yellow Hat Buddhist Monastery, built in 1875 by a Mongolian monk. It houses famous Buddhist scriptures (beautifully displayed) in an interior the colour of the surrounding forests. The austere monastery is a nice walk, at the end of Ghoom's main market street. Also worth visiting is the **Sakyaguru Monastery**, closer to the Darjeeling road, which has 95 monks.

## Tiger Hill
*Shared jeep departs 0430 from Clubside motor stand in Darjeeling Rs 80-100 return.*

If the weather is clear, it is worth rising at 0400 to make the hour's journey to **Tiger Hill** for a breathtaking view of the sunrise on Kangchenjunga. Mount Everest (8846 m), 225 km away, is visible on a good day. The mass of jeeps and the crowds at sunrise disappear by mid-morning. It's a nice walk back from Tiger Hill (about two hours, 11 km) via Ghoom and the **Japanese Peace Pagoda**, where drumming 1630-1900 is worth seeing.

## Listings Darjeeling *map p82*

### Tourist information

#### GTA
*Silver Fir Building, Bhanu Sarani, Mall Rd West, T0354-2255351, www.gtatourism.com, Mon-Sat 1030-1600 (closed 2nd and 4th Sat in month).*
Has brochures and can book GTA-run lodges. There is also a GTA kiosk at Clubside, Laden-La Rd.

#### WBTDC
*Bellevue Hotel, 1st floor, 1 Nehru Rd, T0354-225 4102. Open 1000-1700, off-season 1030-1600.*
Can book state-run tourist lodges, and organizes tours during high season.

### Where to stay

Most hotels are within 2 km of the station and motor stand, a stiff walk uphill. Some top-end hotels include all meals and most offer discounts off season (Jul-Sep, Dec-Feb). Some charge extra for Christmas and New Year. Prices listed are for high season. There is a chronic water shortage, and you may find budget hotels ration their water supply.

#### $$$$ Glenburn Tea Estate
*T(0)9830-070213, www.glenburn teaestate.com.*
Located over an hour from Darjeeling, in a beautiful tea garden. Lots of activities and good walking nearby; gorgeously restored main bungalow and equally attractive newer bungalow, each with 4 unique suites. Dinners

are candlelit, public lounges charming, and the hospitality warm yet refined.

#### $$$$ Windamere
*Observatory Hill, T0354-225 4041/2, www.windamerehotel.com.*
Enviable location, good views when clear, a true relic of the Raj. Spacious rooms and cottages (no phone or TV in some), beware those with dated bathrooms, terraces, chintzy and cluttered with memorabilia, coal fires (can be smoky), hotties in bed, pre-war piano favourites accompany tea. Lounge/bar is a characterful place for a drink, outside guests welcome for high tea (disappointing) or beer. Full-board only.

#### $$$$-$$$ Cedar Inn
*Dr Zakir Hussain Rd, T0354-225 4446, www.cedarinndarjeeling.com.*
Slightly out of town, but great views and free shuttle service throughout the day. Family-friendly, health club, sauna, lovely garden with wrought iron furniture. Wood-panelled rooms are stylish and thoughtfully laid out (bathrooms a bit 1980s), fireplaces in some, public areas with enormous plants, bar and restaurant are welcoming and informal. Extension in same style as the original building. Essential to book in advance.

#### $$$ Darjeeling Gymkhana Resort
*Next to Gymkhana Club, T0354-225 4391, www.darjeelinggymkhanaresort.in.*
Wood-panelled rooms (with fireplaces) are large and modern yet warm and welcoming.

Nice location on Observatory Hill, club on doorstep for sports/activities. Many rooms suited to families and groups. Indian restaurant good, but its position in the central foyer means chatter can be irritating when you're in your room.

### $$$ The Elgin
*HD Lama Rd, T0354-225 7226, www.elginhotels.com.*
Beautifully renovated 125-year-old colonial hotel, rooms full of atmosphere with polished floors, fireplaces, nooks and crannies, yet plush with marble bathrooms. Photos, brass fittings and carpets give warmth to lounge and bar area, like a country sitting room. Tiered garden is flower-filled but looks onto a high fence. All meals included. High tea grossly overpriced for outside guests.

### $$ Bellevue
*Chowrasta, T0354-225 4075, www. bellevuehotel-darjeeling.com.*
Wide range of rooms with bath and geysers, some large, bright and airy (eg rooms 35, 49), some with fireplaces or stoves, all have loads of character with old wooden fittings. Genuinely friendly management. Central located, and the small rooftop has unparalleled K'junga view.

### $$ Classic Guesthouse
*CR Das Rd (below Chowrasta), T0354-225 7025, www.classicguesthouse.in.*
A small quiet guesthouse with a cute lawn, stunning views from the private balcony of each of the 4 large rooms. Plenty of furniture, heaters in winter, carpets, TV, decent big bathrooms. Rooms aren't stylish but they're very comfortable and the manager is nice.

### $$ Planters' Club
*The Mall, T0354-225 4348.*
Aka the 'Darjeeling Club', this wooden building dates from 1868 and oozes history from the curved veranda and creaking balconies. New decor in VIP rooms is

unattractive, a better choice are the 'super' doubles which are dated but have a Raj ambience; huge fireplaces, white-painted furniture, bathrooms feel Victorian. Nice staff and a good place for an evening tipple among moth-eaten animal trophies inside, or out on the terrace (residents only).

### $$ Shangrila
*5 Nehru Rd, T0354-225 4149, www. hotelshangriladarjeeling.com.*
A small and characterful hotel in a good spot near Chowrasta. Large rooms, tastefully renovated, subtly lit, TVs, some with good views from the window seating. new bathrooms, all double beds (no twins, discount for single), 3 rooms have Victorian fireplaces. Excellent restaurant (see page 87).

### $$ Travellers Inn
*Dr Zakir Hussein Rd, T0354-225 8497, www.travellersinndarjeeling.in.*
Very respectable rooms in a modern hotel, hot water, good views from the restaurant with booths, and a sweet indoor 'garden room' that catches any rays of sun.

### $$-$ Dekeling
*51 Gandhi Rd (The Mall), T0354-225 4159, www.dekeling.com.*
Homely rooms are noticeably warm, most have private bath (24-hr hot water), delightful lounge areas with stoves. Range of room tariffs, some attic front rooms with views, 2 doubles with shared bath are a bargain (No 11 is best). Good restaurant, brilliant hosts, reserve ahead (1 month in advance in high season). Noisy when jeeps depart at 0400 for Tiger Hill with lots of hooting.

### $ Aliment
*40 Zakir Hussain Rd, T0354-225 5068, alimentweb98@gmail.com.*
Clean rooms vary in size and cheerfulness, pay more for TV and 24-hr hot shower (otherwise hot water for 2 hrs each evening), cheap singles and triples (hot buckets)

average food in social restaurant (cheap beer), internet, packed with travellers, good atmosphere, excellent library.

### $ Andy's
*102 Zakir Hussain Rd, T0354-225 3125, T(0)9434-166968.*
Airy twin-bed rooms are notable for their cleanliness, some have hot shower or hot buckets provided. Storage for trekkers, friendly and very honest atmosphere if slightly institutional. Discount for single travellers. Often full, ring ahead. No food.

### $ Long Island
*Rockville Dham, Dr Zakir Hussein Rd, near TV tower, T0354-225 2043, pritaya19@yahoo.com.*
Attractive exterior, clean basic rooms, some with private shower (hot water 0800-2000) or share communal bathroom. Appealingly quaint restaurant, quiet location, internet, great views from rooftop and upper rooms. Run by friendly Nepali family. Single room rates.

### $ Pagoda
*1 Upper Beechwood Rd, T0354-225 3498.*
Clean but basic rooms with period furniture in a characterful building, some with bath (limited free bucket hot water), peaceful, good value. Rooms at front better, though not much view from shared balcony. Away from the main backpacker scene and an easier walk from transport links. Very friendly, small library.

### $ Tower View
*Rockville Dham, down the back of TV Tower, T0354-225 4452.*
Pleasant, clean rooms, some with toilet but sharing bathrooms (hot bucket), more expensive with 24-hr hot water, wood stove and dusty book collection in the homely restaurant (a popular place to eat, with a nice back terrace if the weather permits).

### $ Valentino
*6 Rockville Rd, T0354-225 2228, tashiphuntsok30@yahoo.com.*
Clean rooms with a green theme with good mountain views (especially from upper storeys), central heating and 24-hr hot water, good Chinese restaurant, bar, excellent sundeck.

### $ Youth Hostel
*Dr Zakir Hussain Rd, T0354-225 2290.*
Mainly cheap dorm beds, superb position on top of the ridge, no restaurant, trekking information available.

## Restaurants

Hotels with restaurants will usually serve non-residents. Several have bars.

### $$ Glenary's
*Nehru Rd (The Mall), T0354-225 8408.*
Tearoom with excellent confectionery and pastries, friendly, 1st-class breakfast, Kalimpong cheese and wholemeal bread sold. Licensed restaurant upstairs is pricier but lively and with a good atmosphere, bar downstairs has local band on Sat (supposedly 1900-2200 but often finishes early). A Darjeeling 'must'.

### $$ Shangrila
*See Where to stay, page 86.*
Darjeeling's most chic dining experience, contemporary decor mixed with tasteful Tibetan artefacts, and a wide menu of delicious multicuisine food plus bar. Gracious service, open later than most.

### $$-$ Café Coffee Day
*Chowrasta.*
A good spot to watch the world go by with a decent coffee, plus great views from the terrace.

## ON THE ROAD

## Tea in Darjeeling

An ancient Chinese legend suggests that 'tay', or tea, originated in India, although tea was known to have been grown in China around 2700 BC. It is a species of Camellia (*Camellia thea*). After 1833, when its monopoly on importing tea from China was abolished, the East India Company made attempts to grow tea in Assam using wild chai plants found growing there. Tea plants were later introduced to Darjeeling and the Nilgiri hills in the south. Today India is the largest producer of tea in the world. Assam grows over half and Darjeeling about a quarter of the nation's output. Once drunk only by the tribal people, it has now become India's national drink.

The orthodox method of tea processing produces the aromatic lighter coloured liquor of the Golden Flowery Orange Pekoe in its most superior grade. The fresh leaves are dried by fans on withering troughs to reduce the moisture content and then rolled and pressed to express the juices which coat the leaves. These are left to ferment in a controlled environment to produce the desired aroma. Finally the leaves are dried by passing them through a heated drying chamber and then graded – the unbroken being the best quality, down to the fannings and dust. The more common crushing, tearing, curling (CTC) method produces tea which gives a much darker liquor.

Most of Darjeeling's tea is sold through auction houses, the largest centre being in Kolkata. Tea tasting and blending are skills that have developed over a long period of time and are highly prized. The industry provides vital employment in the hill areas and is an assured foreign exchange earner.

There are several tea gardens close to Darjeeling, but not all welcome visitors. Two that do are **Happy Valley Tea Estate** (open Tuesday-Saturday, 0800-1600), about 2 km northeast of the town centre signed off Hill Cart Road, and the **Pattabong Estate** a bit further along the road towards Sikkim.

### $$-$ Lunar
*51 Gandhi Rd, T0354-225 4194.*
*Open from 0730.*
Thoroughly delicious pure veg Indian dishes, and some decent sandwiches, pizzas and Chinese. Modern and informal, family environment, big windows for the view. *Lassis* are fragrant and creamy, service competent and kindly.

### $ Blind Date
*Top floor, Fancy Market, NB Singh Rd,*
*T0354-225 5404. Open 0930-1900.*
Warm and friendly place always packed with locals, cheap Tibetan and Chinese mains, divine soups and clean kitchen in open view, more limited choice for vegetarians.

### $ Dekeva's
*Dekling Hotel, 52 Gandhi Rd, Clubside.*
Nice little place with Tibetan specialities, plus Chinese and Continental, cosy, very popular.

### $ Hasty Tasty
*Nehru Rd.*
Good pure vegetarian fast food, Indian, Chinese, pizzas and sandwiches, popular *thalis* aren't very spicy. Canteen-style service, cheap.

### $ Hot Pizza Place
*HD Lama Rd.*
Genuinely great pizza plus other Western-friendly meals and snacks, one big table holds all-comers. Folks rave about it.

**$ Keventer's**
*Nehru Rd, Clubside.*
This Darjeeling classic has a rooftop, serving snacks, with fabulous views.

**$ Kunga**
*Gandhi Rd. Open 0830-2030.*
Cheerful unpretentious Tibetan joint, with great *momos*, also pizzas and huge backpacker-friendly breakfasts. But it's the range of fantastic soups that are most memorable.

**$ New Dish**
*JP Sharma Rd. Open 0800-1930.*
Chinese. Adventurous menu, mainly Chinese (cheap), excellent chicken entrées, friendly staff. Scruffy aquamarine mirrored walls, serves beer.

**$ Sonam's Kitchen**
*Dr Zakir Hussein Rd.*
Open for breakfast, lunch and dinner (but not in between), Sonam has built up a loyal following for her home-cooking. Menu is limited, service can take a while, but the French toast is a must. Coffee will blow your head off.

### Bars

There are some great options for a *chota peg* in Raj-era surroundings.

Try the **Windamere** (see Where to stay, page 85) with a cosy lounge-feel among knick-knacks, or the **Gymkhana Club** for billiards, worn leather seats and bags of atmosphere. **Joey's Pub**, though housed in an unlikely looking heritage cottage, gathers a rowdy crowd every night for drinks in a true pub ambiance. Surprisingly good typical British bar snacks, very social, open 0930-2300. English-language films show at the **Inox** cinema in Rink Mall.

### Festivals

Apr/May **Buddha Purnima/Jayanti** celebrates the birth of the Buddha in the monasteries.

### Shopping

The markets by the motor stand are colourful and worth visiting.

### Books
**Oxford Bookshop**, *Chowrasta.* Good stock especially local interest: one of West Bengal's best bookshops.

### Handicrafts
Local handicrafts sold widely include Buddhist *tankhas* (hand-painted scrolls surrounded by Chinese brocade), good woodcarving, carpets, hand-woven cloth, jewellery, copper, brass and white metal religious curios such as prayer wheels, bowls and statues. Chowrasta shops are closed on Sun, Chowk Bazar and Middle Bazar on Thu.

**Dorjee** (Laden La Rd). **Eastern Arts** (Chowrasta). **H Mullick**, curios from Chowrasta, a cut above the rest. **Nepal Curios** (Laden La Rd). **Tibetan Refugee Self-help Centre** (see page 83), hand-woven carpets in bold designs and colours, from US$360 including packaging, at least 6-month waiting list.

### Tea
**Nathmull's**, *Laden La Rd (above GPO) and at Rink Mall.* An institution, vast selection (Rs 150-10,000 per kg), avoid fancy packs, knowledgeable owner.

### What to do

### Clubs
**Gymkhana Club**, *T0354-2254342, http://darjeelinggymkhanaclub.com. Open 0700-2200.* For a whole host of activities and sports, indoor and out,

a day at the club is excellent fun. Enquire about temporary membership.

**Planters' Club**, *The Mall, T0354-225 4348.* The old Darjeeling Club, a relic of the Raj, membership (Rs 50 per day for hotel residents only) allows use of pleasant colonial restaurant (buffet meals cost extra), faded but charming bar, billiards, a bit run down but log fires, warm and friendly.

### Mountaineering

**Himalayan Mountaineering Institute**, *T0354-225 4087, www.hmi-darjeeling.com. Office open Mon-Sat 1000-1300.* This famous institute has been training Indian and international mountaineers since 1954. Beginners and advanced courses run for 28 days during the dry months (Mar-May, Sep-Nov). At least 3 months advance registration is required. Details and schedules are given on their website.

### Riding

Pony rides are popular starting at Chowrasta; also possible to do a scenic half-day ride to Ghoom – agree price in writing.

### River rafting

On the Tista, a range of trips from 1½ hrs to 2-day camps with fishing, contact **GTA** (see below).

### Trekking and tours

**Clubside Tours & Travels**, *JP Sharma Rd, T0354-225 5123, http://clubside.in.* Hotel booking, tours, treks, good jeep hire, air tickets for all domestic carriers.

**GTA**, *see page 85.* Runs a variety of tours leaving from the tourist office, including to Mirik, Tiger Hill, Darjeeling town and surrounding areas. Price lists are available at the office.

**Darjeeling Transport Corp**, *30 Laden La Rd.* Maruti vans, jeeps, Land Rovers and a few *sumos* are available. Prices vary according to the season so negotiate rates.

**Himalayan Travels**, *18 Gandhi Rd, T0354-225 2254, http://www.himalayantravels.net.* Long established, good for Sikkim and Singalila treks, tours to Bhutan (need 3-5 days' notice).

**Off Road Adventure**, *http://offroad adventure.in.* Trekking, rafting, rock climbing, kayaking, paragliding are more. Ecologically sound with years of experience.

**Samsara Travel**, *7 Laden-La Rd, T0354-225 2874, www.samsaratourstravelsandtreks.com.* Treks, homestays, village tours, etc.

**Trek-Mate**, *Singalila Arcade, Nehru Rd, T0354-225 6611, trekmatedarj@gmail.com.* Well-equipped trekking agents, English-speaking guides.

### Transport

**Air** Taxi transfer from Bagdogra airport (90 km) takes 3 hrs.

**Bus** Minibuses go from the main transport stand to nearby villages, including **Mirik** at 0825, 0900 and 0925, via **Sukhia** and **Pashupati Fatak** (on the Nepalese border).

**Jeep** Jeeps leave regularly to local destinations. The journeys to Kalimpong and Mirik are particularly stunning, along narrow ridges planted with tea bushes and past wooden villages teetering on precipices. To **Siliguri** from 0600-1630 (2-2½ hrs); to **Gangtok** from 0700-1500 (4-5 hrs); to **Mirik** (2 hrs); to **Kalimpong** from 0700-1600 (2½ hrs); to **Jorethang** from 0800-1500 (Sikkim permit not available at this border, 2 hrs), change at Jorethang for **Pelling**.

**Motorbike** Enfields and other models can be rented from **Adventures Unlimited**,

> **Tip...**
> Pick a jeep that is already over half full, so that you don't have to wait long before setting off. During the high season book a day in advance (particularly to reserve seat No 1).

based in the internet café, opposite Cyber Planet on Zakir Hussein Rd, daily 0830-2000. Around Rs 350 per day.

**Train** Diesel service to **NJP** at 0915, 7½ hrs, 88 km away. A passenger train runs to **Kurseong** (Rs 60/210) via **Ghoom** (Rs 30/140) daily at 1015, taking 3 hrs and returning at 1500. For the tourist-only service to Ghoom, see page 84. The ticket office at the station is open Mon-Sat 0800-1700, Sun 0800-1400, with a break for lunch 1200-1230.

## Trekking around Darjeeling

### challenging trekking on well-used tracks with stunning views

The trekking routes around Darjeeling are well established, having been popular for over 100 years. Walks lead in stages along safe tracks and through wooded hills up to altitudes of 3600 m. Trails pass through small villages, forests and meadows filled with rhododendrons, magnolias, orchids and wild flowers. A stunning backdrop of mountains stretches from Mount Everest to the Bhutan hills, including the third highest mountain in the world, Kanchenjunga. The entire area is a birdwatcher's paradise with more than 600 species, including orioles, minivets, flycatchers, finches, sunbirds, thrushes, piculets, falconets and Hoodson's Imperial pigeons. The mixed rhododendron, oak and conifer forests are particularly well preserved.

## Darjeeling treks

There is an extensive network of varied trails that link the hillside towns and villages. Agents in Darjeeling can organize four- to seven-day treks, providing guide, equipment and accommodation (see Trekking and tours, page 90), though it is perfectly possible to make arrangements on arrival at Manebhanjang, the starting point for the trek.

## Singalila trek

The 160-km Singalila trek passes through the **Singalila National Park** and takes in the highest peak in West Bengal, **Sandakphu** (3636 m). The trek starts from the small border town of **Manebhanjang**, 26 km from Darjeeling. The journey to and from Darjeeling can be done by shared or private jeep in 1½ hours. Walking north to Sandakphu (rather than starting in Sandakphu and heading south) means you are always walking towards the most stunning views. Other possible starting points are: **Dhotrey** (a further hour by jeep, north of Manebhanjang), which cuts out a large chunk of the steep ascent to Tonglu; or **Rimbick**, which means going via Gurdum to Sandakphu. If you have not arranged for transport to meet you at a particular point then it is entirely possible to travel back to Darjeeling from any roadhead by jeep, with services at least once daily, often three to four times daily.

**Day 1 To Tonglu (or Tumling)** 1 km beyond Manebhanjang town you reach a rough stone paved track leading sharply up to the left. Tonglu (3030 m) is 11 km from this point if you follow the jeep track, slightly less if you take the frequent but very steep short cuts. Alternatively, head for Tumling, just the other side of the peak of the hill from Tonglu (you take the alternative road from Meghma and rejoin the main route 1 km after Tumling). There is a

# **Essential** Singalila trek

### Fees

Entry fees for Singalila National Park are paid at the checkpoint in Manebhanjang (foreigners Rs 200, camera Rs 100, video camera Rs 500). In a bid to provide employment for local youth, the West Bengal Forest and Wildlife Department insists that visitors take a guide/porter when entering the Singalila National Park. If you haven't arranged a trek through an agent in Darjeeling, local guides can be hired in Manebhanjang for upwards of Rs 600 per day (although paying more secures someone who speaks good English

### Tip...

Singalila is not an easy trek: several parts are very steep and tough. Even up to May, temperatures at night are freezing and it is essential to take plenty of warm clothes.

### Tip...

If you're staying at a private lodge, be sure to sample hot *chhang*, the local millet brew, served in a wooden keg and sipped through a bamboo straw.

and has a better knowledge of local flora and fauna); porters are Rs 400-500.

### When to go

The best trekking seasons are April to May, when the magnolias and rhododendrons are in full bloom, and October to November when air clarity is best. In spring there may be the occasional shower. In autumn the air is dry and the visibility excellent. In winter the lower altitude trails that link Rimbick with Jhepi (18 km) can be very attractive for birdwatchers.

Trekkers' Hut at **Tonglu** with 24 beds and a fine view of the Kanchenjunga range. From here you can also see the plains of North Bengal and some valleys of Nepal in the distance. Closer to hand are the snow-fed rivers, the Teesta in the east and Koshi in the west. You can also sleep in **Tumling** where **Shikhar Lodge** has simple basic and clean rooms, run by a local teacher's friendly family, "fabulous supper and breakfast" plus a lovely garden. There are tea shops at **Chitre** and at **Meghma**, which has an interesting monastery noted for its large collection of Buddhist statues; (108, according to locals). Ask at the tea house opposite to get in.

**Day 2 To Jaubari and Gairibans** A level walk along the ridge takes you past the long 'mani' wall to the Nepalese village of Jaubari; no visa is needed and good accommodation is available at the **Teacher's Lodge** should you wish to spend a night in Nepal. After Jaubari the trail turns sharply to the right back into Indian territory and down through bamboo and rhododendron forests to the village of Gairibans in a forest clearing. There is a large **Trekkers' Hut** at Gairibans with about 20 beds, or you could carry on all the way to Sandakphu, a long day's hiking.

**Day 3 To Sandakphu** It is 14 km uphill to Sandakphu, with a lunch break in Kalpokhri with its attractive attractive 'black' lake surrounded by fir trees, about midway. Even in winter the lake never freezes. The last 3 km from Bhikebhanjang (tea shop) to Sandakphu are particularly steep; this section takes more than an hour but the views from the Singalila Ridge make it all worthwhile. **Sandakphu**, a small collection of lodges and government buildings, is the the finest viewpoint on the trek and the prime destination for most visitors. Located 57 km from Darjeeling, it is accessible by jeep (the same narrow bumpy track used by trekkers), which is how many Indian tourists make the journey during the season. Sandakphu offers fantastic views, including the eastern face of Everest (8846 m, 140 km away as the crow flies), Kanchenjunga (8586 m), Chomolhari (the highest peak in Bhutan), Lluhe and Makchu (the fourth and fifth highest peaks in the world, respectively) and numerous peaks such as Pandim that lie in Sikkim. A five-minute walk past the towering Sherpa lodge brings you to three hillocks on the left side of the path; the middle one of these is the very highest point at 3636 m.

There is a Trekkers' Hut and several lodges, each with a dining area, toilets and cookhouse. The drive back to Manebhanjang by pre-arranged 4WD can take four hours along the very rough track, if you finish the trek here.

**Day 4 Sandakphu to Phalut** Phalut, 22 km from Sandakphu along an undulating jeepable track, is at the junction of Nepal, Sikkim and West Bengal. It offers even closer views of Kanchenjunga. It is best to avoid trekking here in May and June and mid-September to 25 October when large numbers of college trekking teams from West Bengal descend on the area. From Phalut it's possible to get a jeep back the way you came, via Sandakphu. Alternatively you can walk through the fine forests of the Singalila National Park down to **Rimbick**.

**Day 5 Phalut to Rimbick** From Phalut, walk south for 4 km towards **Bhikebhanjang** and then take the trail towards Rimbick. It takes around four hours to reach **Gorkhey**, which has accommodation, and it's a further 3 km to the village of **Samanden**, hidden in a hanging valley. From Samanden, it is a 6-km walk to **Rammam** where there is a clean, comfortable **Sherpa Lodge** in a tiny garden, recommended for friendly service and good food. Alternatively, the Trekkers' Hut is a 100-m climb (in the direction of Molley) before Rammam village. From Rammam it is a 1½-hour walk down to a couple of private lodges and a Trekkers' Hut at **Siri Khola** and a further 1½ hours to Rimbick. Again, this area has a wealth of birdlife. From Rimbick there are around three jeeps a day to Darjeeling (four hours), or you can return to Manebhanjang via Palmajua and Batasi (80 km).

> **Tip...**
> Although Gorkhey, Phalut, Rammam and Rimbick lie just south of the border with Sikkim, entering Sikkim is not permitted on this route, though agents say this may change in future; ask in Darjeeling about the current situation.

**Days 4/5 alternative route** Sabarkum to Ramman via Molley An alternative quieter trail links Sabarkum (7 km before Phalut on the main Sandakphu–Phalut trail) with Rammam, with a possible overnight stay at the Trekkers' Hut in **Molley**. (Note: the manager of Molley Trekkers' Hut is often to be found at the Forest Office in Sabarkum; look for him on the way through in order to secure a room). From Rammam you could make detour, crossing by a suspension bridge over the Siri Khola River and following the path up the valley to Dentam in Sikkim. This less well-trodden valley has rich birdlife (particularly kingfishers) and excellent views of undisturbed forest.

**Days 6-10 extension** Those with five days to spare can return to Darjeeling by the **Rammam–Rimbick–Jhepi–Bijanbari** route (153 km). From **Bijanbari** (762 m) it is possible to return to Darjeeling, 36 km away by jeep, or climb a further 2 km to Pulbazar and then return to Darjeeling, 16 km away.

## Listings Trekking around Darjeeling

### Where to stay

There are plenty of government trekkers' huts and private lodges of varying standards and prices (on an organized trek these will have been booked for you) at Tonglu, Sandakphu, Phalut, Gorkhey, Molley, Rammam, Rimbick, Siri Khola and other villages. Those at Sandakphu vary widely in standards and price, some costing up to Rs 500 per person with attached bathroom, so it's worth seeing a few. Although room is usually available, it's wise to book in advance during May/Jun and Oct when trails can be very busy. Any trekking agent in Darjeeling can arrange bookings for a small fee. Private lodges, such as Sherpa Lodge in Rimbick and Rammam, and other trailside lodges in Meghma, Jaubari and Kalpokhri, are generally friendly, flexible and provide reasonable basic accommodation. Some places can prepare yak curry on request.

**$$ Karmi Farm**
*North of Bijanbari (access via Kaijali, 4WDs stop 20 mins walk away, or it's 2-3 hrs by pony from Pulbazar), www.karmifarm.com.*
A haven of rural peace at Kolbong, which you may choose to use as a base. 4 doubles with bath, simple but spotless, superb food.

The small low-key hill station of Mirik, at an altitude of 1600 m, has forests of japonica, orange orchards and tea gardens all within easy walking distance. Its restful ambience, dramatic views and homely accommodation make it an appealing stop for a couple of days' relaxation or for good day-trekking.

The focal point is Sumendu Lake encircled by a 3.5-km cobbled promenade that makes a pleasant stroll, and which offers boating and pony rides. Krishannagar, south of the lake, is the main tourist centre while older Mirik Bazar, north of the lake, has a more local vibe. To orientate yourself and plan treks, pick up an excellent map from the Ratnagiri Hotel in Krishnanagar.

### Sights and walks around Mirik

Towering **Bokar Gompa**, a 15-minute uphill walk from the main road in Krishnanagar, is definitely worth visiting (daily chanting at 0530 and 1500). If you continue walking from the monastery, past old Mirik Church and some pretty houses, you reach **Rametay Dara** (Mirik's highest point at 1695 m) with a series of viewpoints across the hills to the plains. Equally impressive are the views to Nepal from the look-out tower at **Kawlay Dara** (east of Mirik), considered best at sunrise but worthwhile at any time. Near here, the tea gardens of the **Thurbo Tea Estate** roll over perfect hillocks and encompass the little **Mahadev Tar Temple** where the mark of Siva's footprint and trident imprint the rocks. Visits to the Thurbo factory can be arranged, ask your hotel for help.

Another excellent walk (four to five hours) goes from the Don Bosco Church (open 0900-1000, 1400-1600) down a new road and stone paths to the *bustee* (village) and tea gardens of **Marma Tea Estate**. From here forest trails and tracks can be followed up and down past orange orchards, squash canes and colourful houses to Mirik Bustee and on to Mirik Bazar. Jeeps ply this route should you become weary; from Marma to Mirik Bazar costs Rs 25. You can even trek to Kurseong (five to six hours) from Marma, going down to the Balasan River to cross a large bridge, and up the winding road on the other side. Or, less ambitiously, take a jeep 6 km up the Darjeeling road and walk back past the rolling Thurbo Tea Estate and little villages of flower-laden cottages.

## Listings Mirik

### Where to stay

The vast majority of accommodation is found in Krishnanagar on the south side of the lake, although there are also 3 hotels in bustling Mirik Bazar on the north side, with a local village atmosphere.

**$$-$ Ratnagiri**
*Krishnanagar, T(0)9832010013,*
*www.hotelratnagiri.com.*

A range of bright spotless rooms, all with bath, some with great views, and a cute garden for breakfast. Discounts for single travellers. The 2 split-level wooden cabins with working fireplaces are lovely. Excellent choice.

**$ Boudi**
*Main Rd, Mirik Bazar, T(0)9932-483476*
*(ask for Nitai).*
The back rooms have stupendous balcony views to Kanchenjunga and are a bargain.

Bright paint, laminate floors, TV, hot water in the morning only, restaurant downstairs. Ask for clean sheets if it's low season – chances are dust will have collected.

**$ Hotel Payal-cum-bar**
*Main Rd, Mirik Bazar, T(0)9734-977541.*
Should the **Boudi** be full, the Payal has cheap singles with hot bucket, and more spacious rooms with geyser, all have TV. The restaurant-cum-bar is well stocked and staff sweet.

**$ Lodge Ashirvad**
*Krishnanagar, T0354-224 3272.*
The best budget option with clean bright rooms, new paint and half-panelling, pay more for geyser, or cheap hot buckets. Rooftop with monastery views and run by a lovely family. Food available during high season.

**$ Tourist Lodge**
*5 mins uphill from the lake, T0354-224 3371.*
Huge wood-panelled rooms, slightly more expensive for suites with balconies (excellent views), standard rooms have carpets (No 102 is best), newly tiled bathrooms, no single room rates, ignore the faded exterior.

### Restaurants

There are extremely cheap *dhabas* near the bus stand offering passable noodle and other dishes. Meals in Mirik Bazar are half the price of Krishnanagar (Boudi Hotel has great veg *momos*).

**$ Blue Lagoon**
*Behind PWD Rest House, near the lake, Krishnanagar. Open 0600-2130.*
Good Indian and Chinese veg and non-veg, served in a pleasant 'hut' with checked tablecloths and windows all around.

**$ Hills Restaurant**
*Near the jeep stand, Main Rd, Krishnanagar. Open from 0700 but closes early.*
Popular little place, with some Indian dishes alongside Tibetan and Chinese, delicious *thukpa*.

**$ Lakeside Restaurant**
*Near the boat shed.*
Pure vegetarian food in a simple little eatery, with a couple of tables outside on the edge of the lake.

**$ Samden**
*Next to Jagjeet Hotel, Main Rd, Krishnanagar. Open 0700-2030 (later than most).*
Great Tibetan food, spicy chai, monks for dining companions.

### Transport

**Jeep** From Krishnanagar, jeeps to **Darjeeling** 0900-1430 (2 hrs); to **Siliguri** every 30 mins 0700-1530 (2 hrs); to **Kurseong** at 1500 (2 hrs); to **Kalimpong** at 0600 (4-5 hrs). Also jeeps to the above destinations from Mirik Bazar, departing 0600-1000. You can reach **Sandakphu** from Mirik; change jeep at **Sukhia**.

**Train** **Mirik Out Agency**, Main Rd, Krishnanagar, can book train tickets to/from NJP.

Kurseong (1450 m) or 'Place of the White Orchid' is a small town worthy of a couple of nights' pause on the way between Siliguri and Darjeeling. (The steam train to Darjeeling leaves every afternoon, supposedly at 1500.) It is famed for its plethora of boarding schools and is surrounded by tea gardens and orange orchards through which there are pleasant walking routes. Locals will sincerely tell you that they call Kurseong "paradise".

### Sights and walks around Kurseong

There are no grand sights in the town, but it is an interesting hike up to the ridge, via St Mary's hamlet (north of the market along Hill Cart Road). Shortcuts past quaint houses and the eerie Forestry College lead up to **St Mary's Well** and **Grotto**, which has fine views and a shrine with candles. Tracks through a young forest reach imposing Dow Hill School, established 1904, and either continue up and over the ridge to tiny Chetri Bustee, or bear right to the little **Forest Museum** at Dow Hill. Head back down via scenically located **Ani Gompa**, housing a small community of nuns belonging to the Red Hat sect, and past pretty cottages. It's around a five-hour walk with stops; ask locals for directions, but double any time frame they give to destinations. Useful sketch maps can be provided by **Cochrane Place** (see Where to stay, below), where it is also possible to arrange guided hikes tailored to match walkers' interests and stamina.

In the town itself there's the narrow and crowded *chowk* market to explore, while a half-hour walk from the railway station brings you to **Eagle's Crag** (shadowed by the TV tower), an awesome vantage point in clear weather.

### Tea estates

The **Makaibari Tea Estate**, 4 km from town, makes an interesting excursion. Dating from 1859 it is India's oldest tea garden, responsibly managed by charismatic Rajah Banerjee who has done much to support the community and initiate environmental and organic development on the estate. The highest price ever fetched at a tea auction was for Makaibari leaves when Rs 18,000 was paid for a kilogram in 2003. Nearby **Ambootia Tea Estate** also conducts factory visits, and from here there's a walk to an ancient Siva temple amid massive Rudraksh and Banyan trees.

## Listings Kurseong

### Where to stay

**$$ Cochrane Place**
*132 Pankhabari Rd, Fatak (2 km from Kurseong on the road to Mirik), T0354-233 0703, www.imperialchai.com.*
Rebuilt and recreated colonial home with rooms crammed with antiques and atmosphere, the personal touch of owner in evidence throughout. Passion fruit grows by balconies, delightful tiered garden, very reasonably priced spa/yoga/ and massage, superlative meals and tea menu (see Restaurants, below). Views of Kanchenjunga from some rooms. Newer annex is cheaper and simpler, with a chalet air. Dorm beds ($) for backpackers. Lovely walking through tea gardens and villages

nearby. Management informative and interesting. Wheelchair access.

### $$-$ Tourist Lodge
*Hill Cart Rd (1 km from station), T0354-234 4409.*
Gloomy corridors but some lovely wooden rooms (check a couple), good views, 24-hr hot water, heaters in winter, snack bar, decent bar and restaurant. Car hire.

### $ Kurseong Palace
*11 Hill Cart Rd, T0354-234 5409, kurseong_palace@yahoo.com.*
Acceptable rooms with TV and carpets, hot water, nice staff.

### $ Makaibari Homestays
*Makaibari, T033-2287 8560, www.makaibari.com.*
Villagers from the tea community provide all meals and a unique experience in their family homes, Western toilets.

## Restaurants

### $$ Chai Country
*At Cochrane Place (see Where to stay, above).*
A meal at Cochrane is not to be missed when in Kurseong. Food is gourmet and inventive, best are the Anglo-Indian dishes with a twist (*dhal* with mint, oyster mushrooms smoked with tea) otherwise African curry, veggie shepherd's pie and more; puddings are exquisite (baked mango).

### $ Abhinandan Fast Food Corner
*Naya Bazar (on way to Eagle's Crag). Open 0900-2030.*

Cubby hole, with character, good veg rolls, *thukpa, momos*.

### $ Gorkha Bhancha Ghar
*At the railway, opposite the platform. Open 0700-1900.*
This specialist *bhancha ghar* (kitchen) serves up cheap and excellent Nepali food in clean surroundings.

### $ Hill Top
*11 TN Rd, T(0)9933-129177.*
Good for Chinese and Tibetan in a cosy restaurant-cum-bar that makes a nod to Chinese decor. Cheap beer.

## What to do

**Voluntary work**
**St Alphonsus Social and Agricultural Centre**, *Tung, near Kurseong, T0354-234 2059, sasac@satyam.net.in.* Run by a Canadian Jesuit, the centre works with the local community through education, housing, agricultural, forestry and marketing projects. They welcome volunteers.

## Transport

**Bus and jeep** Buses and jeeps to **Siliguri**, 1½ hrs and **Darjeeling**, 1 hr, leave from near the railway station; for **Mirik** jeeps leave from Pankhabari Rd.

**Train** The daily diesel service from **NJP** to **Darjeeling** departs at 0900 and reaches Kurseong after 3½ hrs (in theory). From Darjeeling, the train to Kurseong departs at 1015 (1st class Rs 210; 2nd class Rs 60).

**relaxed mountain town with an atmospheric market and beautiful walks**

Set in beautiful wooded mountain scenery with an unhurried air about it, Kalimpong was a meeting point of the once 'Three Closed Lands' on the trade route to Tibet, Bhutan and Nepal. Away from the crowded and scruffy centre near the motor stand, the town becomes more spacious as mountain roads wind up the hillsides leading to monasteries, mission schools and orchid nurseries. The centre is compact enough to be seen comfortably on foot and the surroundings are ideal for walking, though transport is available to visit nearby sights.

From Darjeeling, the 51-km journey (2½ hours) to Kalimpong is through beautiful scenery. The road winds down through tea estates and then descends to 250 m at Tista where it

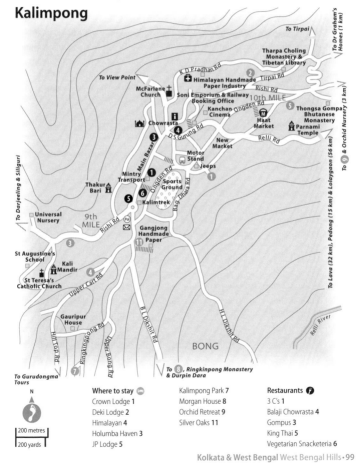

# Kalimpong

| Where to stay | | Kalimpong Park **7** | Restaurants **❼** |
|---|---|---|---|
| Crown Lodge **1** | | Morgan House **8** | 3 C's **1** |
| Deki Lodge **2** | | Orchid Retreat **9** | Balaji Chowrasta **4** |
| Himalayan **4** | | Silver Oaks **11** | Gompus **3** |
| Holumba Haven **3** | | | King Thai **5** |
| JP Lodge **5** | | | Vegetarian Snacketeria **6** |

## BACKGROUND

### People

Today the majority of the people in the state are Bengalis. Tribal groups include Santals, Oraons and Mundas in the plains and the borders of Chota Nagpur, and Lepchas and Bhotias in the Himalaya. The gently rising slopes which lead from the delta to Bihar and Odisha are the home of some of India's most isolated tribal peoples, though their forest habitat has been severely degraded. Over 85% of the population speak Bengali. Hindi, Urdu and tribal languages account for most of the remainder.

crosses the river on a concrete bridge. 'Lovers' Meet' and 'View Point' give superb views of the Rangit and Tista rivers.

### Sights

**Market** The traditional *haat* at 10th Mile has a great atmosphere. Held every Wednesday and Saturday, it draws villagers who come to sell fruit, unfamiliar vegetables, traditional medicines, woollen cloth, yarn and much more. It is remarkably clean and laid back, a delight to explore. Unusual merchandise includes: curly young fern tops, bamboo shoots, dried mushrooms, fragrant spices, musk, *chaang* paraphernalia, large chunks of brown soap, and tiny chickens in baskets alongside gaudy posters.

**Monasteries** There a number of monasteries in and around Kalimpong, the oldest of which, **Thongsa Gompa Bhutanese Monastery** (1692), 10th Mile, has been renovated. The colourful **Tharpa Cheoling Monastery** (1922) has a library of Tibetan manuscripts and *thangkas*. Further nort, is the **Tibetan Monastery** (Yellow Hat) at Tirpai. The **Pedong Bhutanese Monastery** (1837) near the old Bhutanese Damsang Fort at Algara (15 km away) holds ceremonial dances every February.

**Churches** As well as monasteries, there are a couple of old churches worth visiting. The **Macfarlane Church** is close to the town centre, visible from the main street, and built in the Scottish style. **St Theresa's** was built by the Jesuits and resembles a Buddhist *gompa*; it is 2.5 km from the centre in Ninth Mile. Another Scottish church is found at **Dr Graham's Home** on Deolo Hill, www.drgrahamshomes.org. The school was started by the missionary Doctor John Anderson Graham in 1900 when he admitted six Anglo-Indian children. Now there are about 1000 pupils; visitors are welcome to the school as well as the dairy, poultry and bakery projects.

**Paper making** There are two handmade **paper factories** in town, both are small-scale enterprises employing around four people. You can buy their products and watch the paper-making process. **Gangjong Paper Factory** is a short walk from the centre of town, while **Himalayan Handmade Paper Industry** is a good place to stop if walking from Tharpa Chelong Monastery back to Kalimpong; both are open Monday to Saturday 1000-1600.

> **Tip...**
> Some say that the name 'Kalimpong' is derived from *pong* (stronghold) of *kalon* (king's minister), or from *kalibong*, a plant fibre.

**Plant nurseries** Kalimpong excels in producing orchids, amaryllis, roses, cacti, dahlias and gladioli. **Nurseries** include **Ganesh Mani Pradhan** on 12th Mile; **Universal** on Eighth Mile; **Shanti Kunj** on BL Dikshit Road; and **Himalayan** on East Main Road.

> **Tip...**
> Bring a copy of Kiran Desai's *The Inheritance of Loss*, which is set in 1980s Kalimpong during the Gorkha uprising.

### Around Kalimpong

There are pleasant hikes along the Tista Road through rice fields to **Chitray Falls** (9 km), a three-hour walk to **Bhalu Khop**, and a 1½-hour downhill walk from the motor stand to the Relli River. You can picnic on the river beaches at Tista Bazar and Kalijhora.

Further afield, scenic two- to three-hour treks are possible from **Lava**, 32 km east, and **Loleygaon** (also known as **Kaffer village**), 56 km southeast by road via Lava, which has spectacular views of Kangchenjunga. Lava especially is a popular destination for Bengali tourists in the school holidays, with a monastery and weekly market on Tuesday. Both villages are accessible by public jeep/bus from Kalimpong and have reasonably priced private and government accommodation (bookable at the Forest Dept at WBTDC office in Siliguri; see www.wbtdc.com). Walking between the two is a lovely trek of about 10 km. There are other pleasant trails in the vicinity, and generally the walking is fairly level without too many ups and downs. Rhododendrons flower in April around this region.

## Listings Kalimpong *map p99*

### Tourist information

**GTA Reception Centre**
*DB Giri Rd, Damber Chowk, T03552-257992, www.gtatourism.com. Mon-Sat 0930-1700, Sun-1230.*
The tourist office can advise on walking routes and rafting. Also see www.kalimpong.org.

### Where to stay

Discounts offered during winter and monsoon.

**$$$ Silver Oaks**
*Main Rd, T03552-255296, www.elginhotels.com.*
Beautiful rooms of a high standard have a Raj feel, some with fabulous views, buffet restaurant and rather formal bar, gorgeous terraced garden with views from the numerous seating areas.

**$$ Himalayan Hotel**
*Upper Cart Rd, 10-min walk from town centre, T03552-255248, www.himalayanhotel.biz.*
The original stone-built characterful family home of the McDonalds has 8 rooms with traditional furnishings, wooden floors, working fireplaces, no TV, lovely common verandas. 2 well-designed cottages to the rear both have 4 rooms with TV, more modern, trellises and flowers in abundance. Mountain views from the attractive lawn, the restaurant has atmosphere (set menu), comfortable bar with TV, helpful management. One of the oldest hotels in the area (since 1924). Charming.

**$$ Kalimpong Park**
*Ringkingpong Rd, T03552-255304, www.kalimpongparkhotel.com.*
Raj atmosphere aplenty in the 4 good-sized, airy rooms in the Maharaja of Dinajpur's old 2-storeyed house, plus 20 rooms in newer building at rear. Both have new bathrooms

and wooden floors; request a front room as back ones are decidedly gloomy. The $$$ suites are not significantly better, soulless multi-cuisine restaurant but the pleasing bar (see Bars, page 103), large lawn and peaceful location are a big plus. It's a stiff walk from town. Car rental available, Wi-Fi.

### $$ Orchid Retreat
*Ganesh Villa, long walk from town
(4 km from the market), T03552-274517,
www.theorchidretreat.com.*
In an interesting orchid nursery, 6 rooms in traditional thatched cottages (built with local materials) and 4 in a duplex building, hot water (no TV or phone), home-cooked meals, lovely terrace garden with special palm collection, personal attention, peaceful. No walk-ins, must book in advance. Bring your own alcohol.

### $$-$ Holumba Haven
*1 km before the motor stand, 9th Mile,
T03552-256936, www.holumba.com.*
This charming place has 8 cottages (you will struggle to choose between them) spread through a nursery garden, amongst trees and with spacious lawns. Rooms are delightfully decorated, spotless and comfortable (no TVs), with piping hot water and real character. The owners have created a homestay atmosphere and are really friendly and informative. Singles, doubles and triple rooms.

### $ Crown Lodge
*Off Bag Dhara Rd, near Motor Stand,
T03552-255846.*
21 clean well-maintained rooms with hot water (Indian toilets), TV, generator, friendly and helpful, old-style kind of place. Doubles at the back with much light are spacious.

### $ Deki Lodge
*Tirpai Rd, 10 mins uphill from Motor Stand,
T03552-255095, www.kalimpong.org/
dekilodge/index.html.*

Very well-maintained rooms aimed at various budgets, nice terrace restaurant and outdoor seating area, kind and knowledgeable staff, a place with character.

### $ JP Lodge
*RC Mintry Rd, T03552-257457,
www.jplodge.com.*
Clean and simple rooms, charming staff, designated meditation space in a wood-panelled garret (also just a good place to hang out). Rates have increased too much though, and there are no single rates. See the website for details of their homestay, 20 km away in Munsong village.

### $ Morgan House (Kalimpong Tourist Lodge)
*Singamari, Durpin Dara Hill, T03552-255384,
www.wbtdc.gov.in.*
Beautiful location 3 km from centre and a Raj-era building, 7 rooms with bath (good views from upstairs) but run-down and ill-managed, restaurant, bar, gardens.

## Restaurants

Most restaurants shut at 2000. Little restaurants behind the jeep stand dish out delicious *momos* and noodle soups at rock-bottom prices.

### $$ Gompus
*Open 1000-2100.*
Largely meat-based menu, good for Tibetan and Chinese, very popular and a nice environment, alcohol served.

### $$ King Thai
*3rd floor, Maa Supermarket. Open from 0900-2130 (but sometimes till 0200 at weekends).*
Excellent food (more Chinese than Thai, despite the name) attracting a real mix of people. Warmly decorated and professional staff, alcohol served. Live music every night.

**$$-$ 3C's (formerly Glenary's)**
*Main Rd.*
Hangout for local youth, with mainly Western food, breakfast items, great pastries and average coffee. Best for the buzzy vibe rather than the food.

**$ Balaji Chowrasta**
Great choice of vegetarian South/North Indian and Chinese dishes, cheap and good but definitely not glamorous.

**$ Vegetarian Snacketeria**
*Main Rd, opposite Main Bazar.*
Tasty South and North Indian plus a wide choice of drinks.

## Bars

The nicest place for a drink is the bar at the **Kalimpong Park Hotel**, which has a cosy lounge attached and green cane furniture on the small terrace, open until 2100 (beer Rs 130). Also pleasant, though not very pub-like, is the **Himalayan Hotel**.

## Shopping

### Handicrafts

Tibetan and Nepalese handicrafts and woven fabrics are particularly good. There is an abundance of shops on RC Mintry Rd.

**Gangjong**, *Primtam Rd (ask at Silver Oaks Hotel for directions).* Interesting paper factory.
**Soni Emporium**, *near Motor Stand, Mani Link Rd.* Specializes in Himalayan handicrafts.

## What to do

**Gurudongma Tours & Travels**, *T03552-225204.* High-quality, personalized treks, priced accordingly.

## Transport

**Air**  Nearest airport is at Bagdogra (see page 79), 80 km, 2½-3 hrs by taxi. Returning to the airport, you could get a seat in a shared jeep to Bagdogra, then an auto for the last couple of kilometres to the airport.

**Bus and jeep**  Buses use the Bazar Motor Stand. Frequent to **Siliguri/NJP**, 0530-1700 (2½ hrs); **Lava** (2 hrs) and **Kaffer** (3 hrs) at 0800; to **Karkabitta** at 0530 and 1345 (3 hrs); to **Gangtok** at 0730 (3½ hrs). Shared jeeps depart 0630-1500, depending on demand, and are significantly quicker than buses.

**Train**  The nearest mainline railhead is New Jalpaiguri (NJP), 67 km. Tickets are available from **Rly Out Agency**, next to Soni Emporium, Motor Stand, which has computerized bookings and a small tourist quota for trains departing to NJP.

# Practicalities

# Getting there

Kolkata is well connected by air from all over Asia and the Middle East, but there are no direct flights from the UK, Europe or the USA. Many international travellers will arrive in Delhi or Mumbai and take a connecting flight to Kolkata. The international airlines that have the most useful connecting flights to Kolkata from Europe are **Qatar Airways** and **Emirates**, changing in Doha or Dubai. Some carriers permit 'open-jaw' travel, arriving in and departing from different cities in India.

You can fly to numerous destinations across India with **Go Air, Indigo, Jet Airways** or **Spicejet**. The prices are very competitive if domestic flights are booked in conjunction with **Jet** on the international legs. In 2016 the cheapest return flights to Delhi from London started at around £500, but leapt to £900+ as you approached the high seasons of Christmas, New Year and Easter.

**From Europe** Despite the increases to Air Passenger Duty, Britain remains the cheapest place in Europe for flights to India. **Jet Airways, British Airways** and **Air India** fly from London to Delhi or Mumbai in around nine hours. From mainland Europe, major European flag carriers, including **KLM** and **Lufthansa**, fly to Delhi and/or Mumbai from their respective hub airports. In most cases the cheapest flights are with Middle Eastern or Central Asian airlines, transiting via airports in the Gulf. Several airlines from the Middle East (eg **Emirates, Gulf Air, Kuwait Airways, Qatar Airways** and **Oman Air**) offer good discounts to Kolkata and other Indian regional capitals from Europe, but fly via their hub cities, adding to the journey time. Consolidators in the UK can quote some competitive fares, such as: www.skyscanner.net, www.ebookers.com; and **North South Travel** ⓘ T01245-608291, www.northsouthtravel.co.uk (profits to charity).

**From North America** From the east coast, several airlines including **Air India, Jet Airways, Continental** and **Delta** fly direct from New York to Delhi and Mumbai. **American** flies to both cities from Chicago. Discounted tickets on **British Airways, KLM, Lufthansa, Gulf Air** and **Kuwait Airways** are sold through agents although they will invariably fly via their country's capital cities. From the west coast, **Air India** flies from Los Angeles to Delhi and Mumbai, and **Jet Airways** from San Francisco to Mumbai via Shanghai. Alternatively, fly via Hong Kong, Singapore or Bangkok using one of those countries' national carriers. **Air Canada** operates between Vancouver and Delhi. **Air Brokers International** ⓘ www.airbrokers.com, is competitive and reputable. **STA** ⓘ www.statravel.co.uk, has offices in many US cities, as well as Toronto and Ontario. Student fares are also available from **Travel Cuts** ⓘ www.travelcuts.com, in Canada.

**From Australasia** Qantas, Singapore Airlines, Thai Airways, Malaysian Airlines, Cathay Pacific and **Air India** are the principal airlines connecting the continents. **Singapore Airlines** offers the most flexibility, with direct flights to the main Indian cities, through its subsidiary **Silk Air**. Low-cost carriers including **Air Asia** (via Kuala Lumpur) and **Tiger Airways**

(Singapore) offer a similar choice of arrival airports at substantially lower prices, though long layovers and possible missed connections make this a slightly more risky venture than flying with the full-service airlines. **STA** and **Flight Centre** offer discounted tickets from their branches in major cities in Australia and New Zealand. **Abercrombie & Kent** ⓘ *www.abercrombiekent.co.uk*, **Adventure World** ⓘ *www.adventureworld.net.au*, **Peregrine** ⓘ *www.peregrineadventures.com*, and **Travel Corporation of India** ⓘ *www.tcindia.com*, organize tours.

**Airport information** The formalities on arrival in India have been increasingly streamlined during the last few years and the facilities at the major international airports greatly improved. However, arrival can still be a slow process. Disembarkation cards, with an attached customs declaration, are handed out to passengers during the inward flight. The immigration form should be handed in at the immigration counter on arrival. The customs slip will be returned, but must be handed over to customs on leaving the baggage collection hall. You may well find that there are delays of over an hour at immigration in processing passengers who need help with filling in forms. When departing, note that you'll need to have a printout of your itinerary to get into the airport, and the security guards will only let you into the terminal within three hours of your flight. Many airports require you to scan your bags before checking in, and in Kolkata you may also be asked to identify your checked luggage after going through immigration and security checks.

**Departure tax** This is normally included in your international ticket; check when buying. (To save time 'Security Check' your baggage before checking in on departure.) Some airports have also begun charging a Passenger Service Fee or User Development Fee to each departing passenger. This is normally included in international tickets, but some domestic airlines have been reluctant to incorporate the charge. Keep some spare cash in rupees in case you need to pay the fee on arriving at the terminal.

# Getting around

Kolkata's **Subhas Chandra Bose Airport** at Dum Dum receives international and domestic flights. An extensive hub-and-spoke bus operation from Kolkata allows cheap travel within West Bengal and beyond, but long bus journeys in this region are gruelling as roads are generally terrible; use buses only as a last resort when trains are full. Trains link Kolkata with Siliguri in the north of the state, which is the transport hub for the West Bengal Hills, served by Bagdogra Airport and two railway stations (Silguri Junction and New Jalpaiguri or NJP). It is also on NH31, well connected by buses from West Bengal, Assam, Bihar, Sikkim and Bhutan. Darjeeling, Gangtok and Kalimpong are easily reached from Siliguri. Shared jeeps are the best way to get to and around the hills, as they are faster and more frequent than buses and only a little more expensive. Note, however, that roads in the hills can get washed away during the monsoon and may remain in poor condition till October.

## Air

India has a comprehensive network linking the major cities of the different states. Deregulation of the airline industry has had a transformative effect on travel within India, with a host of low-budget private carriers with a host of low-budget private carriers jockeying to provide the lowest prices or highest frequency on popular routes. On any given day, booking a few days in advance, you can expect to fly between Delhi and Kolkata for around US$100 one way including taxes, while a month's notice and flying with a no-frills airline can reduce the price to US$70-80; regional routes, eg Kolkata–Bagdogra or Guwahati, are usually cheaper than routes between main cities.

Competition from the efficiently run private sector has, in general, improved the quality of services provided by the nationalized airlines. The airport authorities, too, have made efforts to improve handling on the ground; major airports are moving towards allowing paperless entry, but you may still need to convert your e-ticket to a paper ticket at the ticket windows outside the terminal.

Although flying is comparatively expensive and has a large environmental impact, for covering vast distances or awkward links on a route it is an option worth considering, though delays can be irritating. For short distances, and on some routes where you can take an overnight sleeper berth (eg Kolkata–Siliguri), it makes more sense to travel by train.

The best way to get an idea of the current routes, carriers and fares is to use a third-party booking website such as www.cheapairticketsindia.com (toll-free numbers: UK T0800-101 0928, USA T1-888 825 8680), www.cleartrip.com, www.makemytrip.co.in, or www.yatra.com. Booking with these is a different matter: some refuse foreign credit cards outright, while others have to be persuaded to give your card special clearance. Tickets booked on these sites are typically issued as an email ticket or an SMS text message – the simplest option if you have an Indian mobile phone, though it must be converted to a paper ticket at the relevant carrier's airport offices before you will be allowed into the terminal. Makemytrip.com and Travelocity.com both accept international credit cards.

**Delays** Be prepared for delays, especially during the winter. In Kolkata and Delhi from early December to February smog is a common morning hazard, sometimes delaying departures by several hours.

## Rail

Trains can still be the cheapest and most comfortable means of travelling long distances saving you hotel expenses on overnight journeys. Rail travel also gives access to booking station Retiring Rooms, basic but usually clean digs within the station which can be a cheap and convenient option for late arrivals or early departures. Above all, you have an ideal opportunity to meet local travellers and catch a glimpse of life on the ground. Remember the dark glass on air-conditioned coaches does restrict vision. See also www.indianrail.gov.in and www.erail.in. A very useful website offering an insight into how to book and navigate the Indian rail network is www.seat61.com.

**High-speed trains** There are air-conditioned 'high-speed' *Shatabdi* (or 'Century') Express for day travel, and *Rajdhani Express* ('Capital City') for overnight journeys. These cover large sections of the network but due to high demand you need to book them well in advance. Meals and drinks are usually included.

**Steam** For rail enthusiasts, the steam-hauled narrow-gauge trains between Kurseong and Darjeeling in northern Bengal is a big attraction and a World Heritage Site. See the IRCTC and **Indian Railways** website, www.irctc.co.in. **SD Enterprises Ltd (SDEL)** ⓘ *www.indiarail.co.uk*, is recommended for tailor-made trips.

**Classes** **A/c First Class**, available only on main routes, has two- or four-berth carpeted sleeper compartments with washbasin. As with all a/c sleeper accommodation, bedding is included, and the windows are tinted to the point of being almost impossible to see through. **A/c Sleeper**, two- and three-tier configurations (known as 2AC and 3AC), are clean and comfortable and popular with middle class families; these are the safest carriages for women travelling alone. **A/c Executive Class**, with wide reclining seats, are available on many *Shatabdi* trains at double the price of the ordinary a/c Chair Car which are equally comfortable. **Second Class (non-a/c)** two- and three-tier (commonly called **Sleeper**), provides exceptionally cheap and atmospheric travel, with basic padded vinyl seats and open windows that allow the sights and sounds of India (not to mention dust, insects and flecks of spittle expelled by passengers up front) to drift into the carriage. On long journeys Sleepers can be crowded and uncomfortable, and toilet facilities can be unpleasant; it is nearly always better to use the Indian-style squat loos rather than the Western-style ones as they are better maintained. At the bottom rung is **Unreserved Second Class**, with hard wooden benches. You can travel long distances for a trivial amount of money, but unreserved carriages are often ridiculously crowded, and getting off at your station may involve a battle of will and strength against the hordes trying to shove their way on.

**Cost** Fares for individual journeys are based on distance covered and reflect both the class and the type of train. For example, a/c First Class three-tier between Kolkata and NJP station costs about Rs 910, and non-a/c Sleeper about Rs 350. Higher rates apply on the *Mail* and *Express* trains and the air-conditioned *Shatabdi* and long-distance *Rajdhani Express*. Children (aged 5-12) travel at half the adult fare. The young (12-30 years) and senior citizens (65 years and over) are allowed a 30% discount on journeys over 500 km (just show your passport). Fares for individual journeys are based on distance covered and reflect both the class and the type of train. Higher rates apply on the *Mail* and *Express* trains and the air-conditioned long-distance *Rajdhani Express*.

**Internet services** Much information is available online via www.railtourismindia.com, www.indianrail.gov.in, www.erail.in and the brilliantly useful www.indiarailinfo.com, where you can check timetables, train numbers, seat availability and even the running status of your train, and even forums discussing the cleanliness, average delay, and food quality of each individual train on the network. Internet e-tickets can be bought and printed on www.irctc.co.in – a great time-saver when the system works properly, though paying with a foreign credit card is fraught with difficulty. If you plan to do a lot of train travel it might be worth the effort to get your credit card recognized by the booking system. This process changes often, so it's good idea is to consult the very active India transport forums at www.indiamike.com. A good option is to seek a local agent who can sell e-tickets, which can cost as little as Rs 10 (plus Rs 20 reservation fee) although some agents charge up to Rs 150 a ticket. This can save hours of hassle; simply present the print-out to the ticket collector. However, it is tricky if you then want to cancel an e-ticket which an agent has bought for you on their account.

**Buying tickets** It's best to book your train tickets as far in advance as possible (currently up to 120 days), as trains on popular routes – and all trains during holiday periods – fill up well ahead of departure. You can reserve tickets for virtually any train on the network from one of the 3000-plus computerized reservation centres across India. To reserve a seat at a booking office, note down the train's name, number and departure time and fill in a reservation form before you line up at the ticket window; you can use one form for up to four passengers. At busy stations the wait can take an hour or more. You can save a lot of time and effort by asking a travel agent to get your tickets for a fee of Rs 50-100. If the class you want is full, ask if tickets are available under any of Indian Rail's special quotas. **Foreign Tourist Quota** (FTQ) reserves a small number of tickets on popular routes for overseas travellers; you need your passport and either an exchange certificate or ATM receipt to book tickets under FTQ. Fairlie Place in central Kolkata has a **Foreign Tourist Counter** where you can buy FTQ tickets; if you are first through the doors in the morning then the process can be swift and smooth (see page 61 for further details on Fairlie). The other useful special quota is Tatkal, which releases a last-minute pool of tickets on the day before the train departs: at 1000 for AC classes and 1100 for non-AC. If the quota system can't help you, consider buying a 'wait list' ticket, as seats often become available close to the train's departure time; you can check your wait list status at via SMS or phone the station on the day of departure to check your ticket's status.

**Rail travel tips** **Bedding**: It can get cold in air-conditioned coaches when travelling at night. Bedding is provided on second class air-conditioned sleepers. On others it can be hired for Rs 30 from the Station Baggage Office for second class.

    **Berths**: It is worth asking for upper berths, especially in second-class three-tier sleepers, as they can also be used during the day when the lower berths are used as seats. Once the middle berth is lowered for sleeping the lower berth becomes too cramped to sit on. Passengers with valid tickets but no berth reservations are sometimes permitted to travel overnight, causing great discomfort to travellers occupying lower berths.

**Delays**: Delays are common on all types of transport, and it's vital to allow plenty of time for making connections. The special *Rajdhani Express* is quite reliable, and the overnight trains to NJP station (for onward travel to Darjeeling and the hills) generally leave Kolkata on time. Ordinary *Express* and *Mail* trains have priority over local services, but generally the longer the journey time, the greater the delay. Delays on the rail network are cumulative, so arrivals and departures from mid-stations are often several hours behind schedule. Allow at least two hours for connections, more if the first part of the journey is long distance. Food and drink: It is best to carry some, though tea, bottled water and snacks are sold on trains and platforms. Carry plenty of small notes and coins on long journeys. On long-distance trains, the restaurant car is often near the upper-class carriages.

**Ladies' compartments**: A woman travelling alone, overnight, on an unreserved second-class train can ask if there is one of these. Lone female travellers may feel more comfortable in air-conditioned sleeper coaches, which require reservations and are used by Indian families.

**Ladies' and seniors' queues**: Separate (much shorter) ticket queues may be available for women and senior citizens.

**Left luggage**: Bags can be left for up to 30 days in station cloakrooms. These are especially useful when there is time to go sightseeing before an evening train. The bags must be lockable and you are advised not to leave any food in them.

**Overbooking**: Passengers with valid tickets but no berth reservations are sometimes permitted to travel overnight, causing great discomfort to travellers occupying lower berths. Wait-listed passengers should confirm the status of their ticket in advance by calling enquiries at the nearest computerized reservation office. If you have access to www.irctc.in you can also check the waitlist status of your ticket using the PNR number or a travel agent can do this online. At the station, check the reservation charts (usually on the relevant platform) and contact the Station Manager or Ticket Collector.

**Porters**: These can carry prodigious amounts of luggage. Rates vary from station to station (sometimes listed on a board on the platform) but are usually around Rs 10-25 per item of luggage. Establish the rate first.

**Pre-paid taxis**: Many main stations have a pre-paid taxi (or auto-rickshaw) service which offers a reliable service at a fair price. If there are no pre-paid taxis ask your hotel for a guide price.

**Security**: Keep valuables close to you, securely locked, and away from windows. For security, carry a good lock and chain to attach your luggage.

**Timetables** Regional timetables are available cheaply from station bookstalls; the monthly *Indian Bradshaw* is sold in principal stations. The handy *Trains at a Glance* (Rs 40) lists popular trains likely to be used by most foreign travellers and is available at stalls at railway stations.

## Road

Road travel is often the only choice for reaching many of the places of outstanding interest in which East India is so rich. For the uninitiated, travel by road can also be a worrying experience because of the apparent absence of conventional traffic regulations. Driving in the mountains can also be nerve-wracking, especially during the rainy season when landslides are possible. Vehicles drive on the left – in theory. Routes around the major cities are usually crowded with lorry traffic, especially at night, and the main roads are often poor and slow. There are a few motorway-style expressways, but most main roads are single track. Some district roads are quiet, and although they are not fast they can be a good way of seeing the country and village life if you have the time.

### Bus

Buses reach virtually every part of West Bengal, offering a cheap, if often uncomfortable, means of visiting places off the rail network. Very few villages are now more than 2-3 km from a bus stop. Services are run by the State Corporation from a city or town's State Bus Stand, while private bus companies often have offices nearby. The latter allow advance reservations, including booking printable e-tickets online (check www.redbus.in and www.viaworld.in) and, although tickets prices are a little higher, they have fewer stops and are a bit more comfortable. In the absence of trains, buses are often the only budget option. There are some sleeper buses (a contradiction in terms) running up to Siliguri – if you must take a sleeper bus, choose a lower berth near the front of the bus. The upper berths are almost always really uncomfortable on bumpy roads.

**Bus categories** Though comfortable for sightseeing trips, apart from the very best 'sleeper coaches' even **air-conditioned luxury coaches** can be very uncomfortable for really long journeys. Often the air conditioning is very cold so wrap up. Journeys over 10 hours can be extremely tiring so it is better to go by train if there is a choice. **Express buses** run over long distances (frequently overnight), these are often called 'video coaches' and can be an appalling experience unless you appreciate loud film music blasting through the night. Ear plugs and eye masks may ease the pain. They rarely average more than 45 kph. **Local buses** are often very crowded, quite bumpy, slow and usually poorly maintained. However, over short distances, they can be a very cheap, friendly and easy way of getting about. Even where signboards are not in English someone will usually give you directions. Many larger towns have **minibus** services which charge a little more than the buses and pick up and drop passengers on request. Again very crowded, and with restricted headroom, they are the fastest way of getting about many of the larger towns.

**Bus travel tips** Some towns have different bus stations for different destinations. Booking on major long-distance routes is now computerized. Book in advance where possible and avoid the back of the bus where it can be very bumpy. If your destination is only served by a local bus you may do better to take the Express bus and 'persuade' the driver, with a tip in advance, to stop where you want to get off. You will have to pay the full fare to the first stop beyond your destination but you will get there faster and more comfortably. When an unreserved bus pulls into a bus station, there is usually an unholy scramble for seats, whilst those arriving have to struggle to get off! In many areas there is an unwritten 'rule of reservation' using handkerchiefs or bags thrust through the windows to reserve seats. Some visitors may feel a more justified right to a seat having fought their way through the crowd, but it is generally best to do as local people do and be prepared with a handkerchief or 'sarong'. As soon as it touches the seat, it is yours! Leave it on your seat when getting off to use the toilet at bus stations.

## Car

A car provides a chance to travel off the beaten track, and gives unrivalled opportunities for seeing something of India's great variety of villages and small towns. Until recently, the most widely used hire car was the Hindustan Ambassador. However, except for the newest model, they are often very unreliable, and although they still have their devotees, many find them uncomfortable for long journeys. For a similar price, Maruti cars and vans (Omni), and Tata and Toyota models (with mod-cons like air conditioning and seat belts) are more reliable and are now the preferred choice in many areas. Gypsy 4WDs and Jeeps are also available, especially in the hills, where larger Sumos make an appearance. A handful of international agencies offer self-drive car hire (**Avis**, **Sixt**), but India's anarchic traffic culture is not for the faint-hearted. It's much morecommon, and comfortable, to hire not just the car but someone to drive it for you.

**Car travel tips** When booking emphasize the importance of good tyres and general roadworthiness. On main roads across India petrol stations are reasonably frequent, but some areas are poorly served. Some service stations only have diesel pumps though they may have small reserves of petrol. Always carry a spare can. Diesel is widely available and normally much cheaper than petrol. Petrol is rarely above 92 octane. Drivers must have third-party insurance. This may have to be with an Indian insurer, or with a foreign insurer who has a national guarantor. You must also be in possession of an International Driving Permit, issued by a recognized driving authority in your home country (eg the AA in the UK, apply at least six weeks before leaving). Asking the way can be very frustrating as you are likely to get widely conflicting advice each time you stop to ask (this happens to Indians asking directions too, it's not just a game to play on foreigners!). On the main roads, 'mile' posts periodically appear in English and can help. Elsewhere, it is best to ask directions often and follow the average direction. Accidents often produce large and angry crowds very quickly. It is best to leave the scene of the accident and report it to the police as quickly as possible thereafter. Ensure that you have adequate provisions, plenty of food and drink and a basic tool set in the car.

**Car hire** Hiring a car and driver is the most comfortable and efficient way to cover short to medium distances, and although prices have increased sharply in recent years car travel in India is still a bargain by Western standards. A car shared by three or four people is very good value, and even if you're travelling on a modest budget a day's car hire can help take the sting out of an arduous journey, allowing you to go sightseeing along the way without looking for somewhere to stash your bags. Be sure to check carefully the mileage at the beginning and end of the trip. Two- or three-day trips from main towns can also give excellent opportunities for sightseeing off the beaten track in reasonable comfort.

Local drivers often know their way much better than drivers from other states, so where possible it is a good idea to get a local driver who speaks the state language, in addition to being able to communicate with you. The best way to guarantee a driver who speaks good English is to book in advance with a professional travel agency, either in India or in your home country. You can, if you choose, arrange car hire informally by asking around at taxi stands, but don't expect your driver to speak anything more than rudimentary English. In the mountains, it is better to use a driver who knows the roads. On pre-arranged overnight trips the fee you pay will normally include fuel and interstate taxes – check before you pay – and a wage for the driver. Some tourist hotels provide rooms for drivers, but they often choose to sleep in the car overnight to save money. They are responsible for their own expenses, including meals. In some areas, drivers also seek to increase their earnings by taking you to hotels and shops where they earn a handsome commission; these are generally hugely overpriced and poor alternatives to the hotels recommended in this book, so don't be afraid to say no and insist on your choice of accommodation. If you feel inclined, a tip at the end of the tour of Rs 100 per day in addition to their daily allowance is appropriate. Be sure to check carefully the mileage at the beginning and end of the trip.

|  | Tata Indica<br>non-a/c | Tata Indigo<br>non-a/c | Hyundai<br>Accent a/c | Toyota<br>Innova |
| --- | --- | --- | --- | --- |
| 8 hrs/80 km | Rs 1200 | Rs 1600 | Rs 2200 | Rs 2500 |
| Extra km | Rs 8 | Rs 10 | Rs 15 | Rs 15 |
| Extra hour | Rs 80 | Rs 100 | Rs 200 | Rs 180 |
| **Out of town** |  |  |  |  |
| Per km | Rs 8 | Rs 10 | Rs 15 | Rs 15 |
| Night halt | Rs 200 | Rs 200 | Rs 300 | Rs 250 |

## Taxi

Taxi travel in India is a great bargain, and in Kolkata you can take a taxi from the airport to the centre for under US$10. Yellow-top taxis in cities and large towns are metered, although tariffs change frequently. In Kolkata, these changes are shown on a fare chart which should be read in conjunction with the meter reading. Increased night time rates apply, and there might be a small charge for luggage. Insist on the taxi meter being flagged in your presence. If the driver refuses, the official advice is to contact the police. This may not work, but it is worth trying. When a taxi doesn't have a meter, you will need to fix the fare before starting the journey. Ask at your hotel desk for a guide price. As a foreigner, it is rare to get a taxi in the big cities to use the meter – if they are eager to, watch out as sometimes the meter is rigged and they have a fake rate card. Also, watch out for the David Blaine-style note shuffle: you pay with a Rs 500 note, but they have a Rs 100 note in their hand.

Most airports and major stations have booths where you can book a prepaid taxi. For slightly more than the metered fare these allow you to sidestep overcharging and give you the security of knowing that your driver will take you to your destination by the most direct route. You might be able to join up with other travellers at the booth to share a taxi to your hotel or a central point. It's OK to give the driver a small tip at the end of the journey. At night, always have a clear idea of where you want to go and insist on being taken there. Taxi drivers may try to convince you that the hotel you have chosen 'closed three years ago' or is 'completely full'. Insist that you have a reservation.

### Rickshaw

**Auto-rickshaws** (autos) are almost universally available in towns across West Bengal and are a cheap and convenient way of getting about. It is best to walk a short distance away from a hotel gate before picking up an auto to avoid paying an inflated rate. In addition to using them for short journeys it is often possible to hire them by the hour, or for a half- or full-day's sightseeing. In some areas younger drivers who speak some English and know their local area well may want to show you around. However, rickshaw drivers are often paid a commission by hotels, restaurants and gift shops so advice is not always impartial. Drivers generally refuse to use a meter, often quote a ridiculous price or may sometimes stop short of your destination. If you have real problems it can help to note down the vehicle licence number and threaten to go to the police.

**Cycle-rickshaws** and **horse-drawn tongas** are more common in small towns or the outskirts of a large one. You will need to fix a price by bargaining. The animal attached to a tonga usually looks too undernourished to have the strength to pull the driver, let alone passengers. Kolkata is the only place in India where you will still see hand-pulled rickshaws, particularly around the New Market area and narrow streets of north Kolkata. They can be useful as a means of covering short distances and are invaluable during the monsoon, but you will need to haggle fiercely and still be prepared to pay above the odds.

# Essentials A-Z

## Accident and emergency

Contact the relevant emergency service (police T100, fire T101, ambulance T102) and your embassy. Make sure you obtain police/medical reports required for insurance claims.

## Customs and duty free

Tourists are allowed to bring in all personal effects 'which may reasonably be required', without charge. The official customs allowance includes 200 cigarettes or 50 cigars, 0.95 litres of alcohol, a camera and a pair of binoculars. Valuable personal effects and professional equipment including jewellery, special camera equipment and lenses, laptop computers and sound and video recorders must be declared on a **Tourist Baggage Re-Export Form (TBRE)** in order for them to be taken out of the country, though in practice it's relatively unlikely that your bags will be inspected beyond a cursory X-ray. These forms require the equipment's serial numbers. It saves considerable frustration if you know the numbers in advance and are ready to show them on the equipment. In addition to the forms, details of imported equipment may be entered into your passport. Save time by completing the formalities while waiting for your baggage. It is essential to keep these forms for showing to the customs when leaving India, otherwise considerable delays are very likely at the time of departure.

### Currency regulations

There are no restrictions on the amount of foreign currency or TCs a tourist may bring into India. If you are carrying more than US$5000 in cash or US$10,000 or its equivalent in cash and TCs you need to fill in a currency declaration form. This could change with a relaxation in the currency regulations.

If you are travelling to Nepal, note that it is illegal to take Indian Rs 500 and Rs 1000 notes into the country. These notes will be confiscated, and offenders are liable to fines or imprisonment.

### Prohibited items

The import of dangerous drugs, live plants, gold coins, gold and silver bullion and silver coins not in current use are either banned or subject to strict regulation. It is illegal to import firearms into India without special permission. Enquire at consular offices abroad for details.

## Drugs

Certain areas have become associated with foreigners who take drugs. These are likely to attract local and foreign drug dealers, but be aware that the government takes the misuse of drugs very seriously. Anyone charged with the illegal possession of drugs risks facing a fine of Rs 100,000 and a minimum 10 years' imprisonment. Several foreigners have been imprisoned for drugs-related offences in the last decade.

## Electricity

India's supply is 220-240 volts AC. Some top hotels have transformers. There may be pronounced variations in the voltage, and power cuts are common. Power back-up by generator or inverter is becoming more widespread, even in humble hotels, though it may not cover a/c. Socket sizes vary so take a universal adaptor; low-quality versions are available locally. Many hotels, even in the higher categories, don't have electric razor sockets. Invest in a stabilizer for a laptop.

## Embassies and consulates

For information on visas and immigration, see page 124. For a comprehensive list of embassies (but not all consulates), see www.immihelp.com or http://embassy.goabroad.com.

## Festivals

### The Hindu calendar

Hindus follow 2 distinct eras: The Vikrama Samvat which began in 57 BC and the Salivahan Saka which dates from AD 78 and has been the official Indian calendar since 1957. The Saka new year starts on 22 Mar and has the same length as the Gregorian calendar. The 29½-day lunar month with its 'dark' and 'bright' halves based on the new and full moons, are named after 12 constellations, and total a 354-day year. The calendar cleverly has an extra month (adhik maas) every 2½ to 3 years, to bring it in line with the solar year of 365 days coinciding with the Gregorian calendar of the West.

Some major regional festivals are listed below. A few count as national holidays: 26 Jan: Republic Day; 15 Aug: Independence Day; 2 Oct: Mahatma Gandhi's Birthday; 25 Dec: Christmas Day.

### Major festivals and fairs

**Jan** New Year's Day (1 Jan) is accepted officially when following the Gregorian calendar. There are regional variations that fall on different dates, often coinciding with spring/harvest time in Mar and Apr.

**14 Jan** Makar Sankranti, also known as **Poush Sankranti** in West Bengal, marks the end of winter and is celebrated with special sweets.

**Feb** Vasant Panchami, a spring festival when people wear yellow clothes to mark the season, is known as **Saraswati Puja** in West Bengal and honours the goddess of learning. Idols of Saraswati are taken on procession before being immersed in the river.

**Feb-Mar** Maha Sivaratri marks the night when Siva danced his celestial dance of destruction (Tandava), which is celebrated with feasting and fairs at Siva temples, but preceded by a night of devotional readings and hymn singing.

**Mar** Holi, the festival of colours, marks the climax of spring. The previous night bonfires are lit symbolizing the end of winter (and conquering of evil). People have fun throwing coloured powder and water at each other and in the evening some gamble with friends. If you don't mind getting covered in colours, you can risk going out – but celebrations can sometimes get very rowdy (and unpleasant).

**15 Apr** Poila Boishakh, Bengali New Year.
**Apr/May** Buddha Jayanti, the 1st full moon night in Apr/May marks the birth of the Buddha.

**Jul/Aug** Rakhi (or Raksha) Bandhan symbolizes the bond between brother and sister, celebrated at full moon. A sister says special prayers for her brother and ties coloured threads around his wrist to remind him of the special bond. He in turn gives a gift and promises to protect and care for her.

**15 Aug** Independence Day, a national secular holiday is marked by special events.

**Aug/Sep** Janmashtami, the birth of Krishna is celebrated at midnight at Krishna temples.

**Sep/Oct** Dasara has many local variations. In the east, it takes the form of **Durga Puja** and is the biggest annual festival in Kolkata and throughout West Bengal. Celebrations for the 10 nights focus on Durga's victory over the demon Mahishasura. Huge pandals (bamboo marquees) are constructed throughout the city, some are traditional while others represent current popular trends, and the streets are completely packed all night long). 2 weeks later is

**Kali Puja**, not quite as intense and all-encompassing, but still fascinating.

**Oct/Nov** **Gandhi Jayanti** (2 Oct), Mahatma Gandhi's birthday, is remembered with prayer meetings and devotional singing.

**Diwali/Deepavali** (Sanskrit ideepa lamp) is the festival of lights. Some Hindus celebrate Krishna's victory over the demon Narakasura, some Rama's return after his 14 years' exile in the forest when citizens lit his way with oil lamps. The festival falls on the dark chaturdasi (14th) night (the one preceding the new moon), when rows of lamps or candles are lit in remembrance, and rangolis are painted on the floor as a sign of welcome. Fireworks have become an integral part of the celebration which are often set off days before Diwali. Equally, Lakshmi, the Goddess of Wealth (as well as Ganesh) is worshipped by merchants and the business community who open the new financial year's account on the day. Most people wear new clothes; some play games of chance.

**Guru Nanak Jayanti** in Nov commemorates the birth of Guru Nanak. Akhand Path (unbroken reading of the holy book) takes place and the book itself (Guru Granth Sahib) is taken out in procession.

**Dec** **Christmas Day** (25 Dec) sees Indian Christians celebrate the birth of Christ in much the same way as in the West; many churches hold services/mass at midnight. There is an air of festivity in city markets which are specially decorated and illuminated.

#### Muslim holy days

These are fixed according to the lunar calendar. According to the Gregorian calendar, they tend to fall 11 days earlier each year, dependent on the sighting of the new moon.

**Ramadan** is the start of the month of fasting when all Muslims (except young children, the very elderly, the sick, pregnant women and travellers) must abstain from food and drink, from sunrise to sunset.

**Id ul Fitr** is the 3-day festival that marks the end of Ramadan.

**Id-ul-Zuha/Bakr-Id** is when Muslims commemorate Ibrahim's sacrifice of his son according to God's commandment; the main time of pilgrimage to Mecca (the Hajj). It is marked by the sacrifice of a goat, feasting and alms giving.

**Muharram** is when the killing of the Prophet's grandson, Hussain, is commemorated by Shi'a Muslims. Decorated tazias (replicas of the martyr's tomb) are carried in procession by devout wailing followers who beat their chests to express their grief. Murshidabad is noted for its grand tazias. Shi'as fast for the 10 days.

### Health

Local populations in India are exposed to a range of health risks not encountered in the Western world. Many of the diseases are major problems for the local poor and destitute and, although the risk to travellers is more remote, they cannot be ignored. Obviously 5-star travel is going to carry less risk than backpacking on a budget.

Healthcare in the region is varied. There are many excellent private and government clinics/hospitals. As with all medical care, first impressions count. It's worth contacting your embassy or consulate on arrival and asking where the recommended (ie those used by diplomats) clinics are. You can also ask about locally recommended medical dos and don'ts. If you do get ill, and you have the opportunity, you should also ask your medical insurer whether they are satisfied that the medical centre/hospital you have been referred to is of a suitable standard.

#### Before you go

Ideally, you should see your GP or travel clinic at least 6 weeks before your departure for general advice on travel risks, malaria and vaccinations. Make sure you have travel insurance, get a dental check (especially if you are going to be away for more than a month), know your own blood group and if you suffer a long-term condition such as diabetes or epilepsy make sure someone knows or that you have a **Medic Alert** bracelet/necklace with this information on it. Remember that it is risky to buy medicinal tablets abroad because the doses may differ and India has a huge trade in false drugs.

## Vaccinations

If you need vaccinations, see your doctor well in advance of your travel. Most courses must be completed at least 4 weeks before you go. Travel clinics may provide rapid courses of vaccination, but are likely to be more expensive. The following vaccinations are recommended: typhoid, polio, tetanus, infectious hepatitis and diptheria. For details of malaria prevention, contact your GP or local travel clinic.

The following vaccinations may also be considered: rabies, possibly BCG (since TB is still common in the region) and in some cases meningitis and diphtheria (if you're staying in the country for a long time). Yellow fever is not required in India but you may be asked to show a certificate if you have travelled from Africa or South America. Japanese encephalitis may be required for rural travel at certain times of the year (mainly rainy seasons). An effective oral cholera vaccine (Dukoral) is now available as 2 doses providing 3 months' protection.

## If you get ill

Contact your embassy or consulate for a list of doctors and dentists who speak your language, or at least some English. Good-quality healthcare is available in the larger centres but it can be expensive, especially hospitalization. Make sure you have adequate insurance. You can also ask at your hotel for good local doctors.

### Kolkata medical services

**Apollo Gleneagles Hospital**, 5B Canel Circular Rd, T033-2320 3040/2122, www.apollogleneagles.in. **Woodlands Hospital**, 8B Alipore Rd, T033-2456 7075-9, www.woodlandshospital.in.

### Websites

**Blood Care Foundation (UK), www.bloodcare.org.uk** A charity that will dispatch certified non-infected blood of the right type to your hospital/clinic.
**British Global Travel Health Association (UK), www.bgtha.org** An organization of travel health professionals.
**Fit for Travel, www.fitfortravel.scot.nhs.uk** A quick A-Z of vaccine and travel health advice requirements for each country.
**Foreign and Commonwealth Office (FCO) (UK), www.fco.gov.uk** A key travel advice site, with useful information on the country, people, climate and lists the UK embassies/consulates.
**The Health Protection Agency, www.hpa.org.uk** Up-to-date malaria advice guidelines for travel around the world.
**Medic Alert (UK), www.medicalalert.com** The foundation that produces bracelets and necklaces for those with existing medical problems.
**World Health Organisation, www.who.int** This lists the diseases in different regions of the world.

## Language

Hindi, spoken as a mother tongue by over 400 million people, is India's official language. The use of English is also enshrined in the Constitution for a wide range of official purposes, notably communication between Hindi and non-Hindi speaking states. In West Bengal more than 85% of the population speak Bengali, 5% speak Urdu, and in Darjeeling district people of Nepali descent speak Gorkhali/Nepali.

English plays an important role across India. It is widely spoken in towns and cities and even in quite remote villages it is usually not difficult to find someone who speaks at least a little English. Outside of major tourist sites, other European languages are almost completely unknown. The accent in which English is spoken is often affected strongly by the mother tongue of the speaker and there have been changes in common grammar which sometimes make it sound unusual. Many of these changes have become standard Indian English usage, as valid as any other varieties of English used around the world.

## Money

Indian currency is the Indian Rupee (Re/Rs). It is **not** possible to purchase these before you arrive. If you want cash on arrival it is best to get it at the airport bank, although see if an ATM is available as airport rates are not very generous. Rupee notes are printed in denominations of Rs 1000, 500, 100, 50, 20, 10. The rupee is divided into 100 paise. Coins are minted in denominations of Rs 10, Rs 5, Rs 2, Rs 1 and (the increasingly uncommon) 50 paise. **Note** Carry money, in a money belt worn under clothing. Have a small amount in an easily accessible place.

### Exchange rates
*UK £1 = Rs 94.2, €1 = Rs 75.2, US$1 = Rs 66.2 (Apr 2016).*

### ATMs
By far the most convenient method of accessing money, ATMs are all over India, usually attended by security guards, with most banks offering some services to holders of overseas cards. Banks whose ATMs will issue cash against Cirrus and Maestro cards, as well as Visa and MasterCard, include, Citibank, HDFC, HSBC, ICICI, IDBI, **State Bank of India (SBI)**, **Standard Chartered** and **UTI**. A withdrawal fee is usually charged by the issuing bank on top of the conversion charges applied by your own bank. Fraud prevention measures quite often result in travellers having their cards blocked by the bank when unexpected overseas transactions occur; advise your bank of your travel plans before leaving.

### Credit cards
Major credit cards are increasingly acceptable in the main centres, though in smaller cities and towns it is still rare to be able to pay by credit card. Payment by credit card can sometimes be more expensive than payment by cash, whilst some credit card companies charge a premium on cash withdrawals. **Visa** and **MasterCard** have an ever growing number of ATMs in major cities and several banks offer withdrawal facilities for Cirrus and Maestro cardholders. It is however easy to obtain a cash advance against a credit card. Railway reservation centres in major cities take payment for train tickets by Visa card which can be very quick as the queue is short, although they cannot be used for Tourist Quota tickets.

### Currency cards
If you don't want to carry lots of cash, pre-paid currency cards allow you to preload money from your bank account, fixed at the day's exchange rate. They look like a credit or debit card and are issued by specialist money changing companies, such as **Travelex** and **Caxton FX**. You can top up and check your balance by phone, online and sometimes by text.

### Changing money
The **State Bank of India** and several others in major towns are authorized to deal in foreign exchange. Some give cash against Visa/MasterCard (eg. ANZ). The larger cities have licensed money changers with offices

usually in the commercial sector. Changing money through unauthorized dealers is illegal. Premiums on the currency black market are very small and highly risky. Large hotels change money 24 hrs a day for guests, but authorised money changers and banks often give a substantially better rate of exchange. Many international flights arrive during the night and it is generally far easier and less time consuming to change money at the airport than in the city. You should be given a foreign currency encashment certificate when you change money through a bank or authorized dealer; ask for one if it is not automatically given. It allows you to change Indian rupees back to your own currency on departure. It also enables you to use rupees to pay hotel bills or buy air tickets for which payment in foreign exchange may be required. The certificates are only valid for 3 months.

## Cost of living

The cost of living in India remains well below that in the West. The average wage per capita is about Rs 68,700 per year (US$1200). Manual, unskilled labourers (women are often paid less than men), farmers and others in rural areas earn considerably less. However, thanks to booming global demand for workers who can provide cheaper IT and technology support functions and many Western firms transferring office functions or call centres to India, salaries in certain sectors have increased dramatically. An IT specialist can earn an average Rs 500,000 per year and upwards – a rate that is rising by around 15% a year.

## Cost of travelling

Most food, accommodation and public transport, especially rail and bus, is exceptionally cheap, although basic food items such as rice, lentils, tomatoes and onions have skyrocketed. There is a widening range of moderately priced but clean hotels and restaurants outside the big cities, making it possible to get a great deal for your money. Budget travellers sharing a room, taking public transport, avoiding souvenir stalls, and eating nothing but rice and dhal can get away with a budget of Rs 600-800 (about US$9-12 or £6-8) a day. This sum leaps up if you drink alcohol (still cheap by European standards at about US$2, £1 or Rs 80 for a bottle), smoke foreign-brand cigarettes or want to have your own wheels (you can expect to spend Rs 250-400 to hire a scooter per day). Those planning to stay in fairly comfortable hotels and use taxis sightseeing should budget at US$50-80 (£30-50) a day. On the other hand, you could check into the **Oberoi Grand** or the **Taj Bengal** for Christmas and notch up an impressive US$600 (£350) bill on your B&B alone. India can be a great place to pick and choose, save a little on basic accommodation and then treat yourself to the type of meal you could only dream of affording back home. A newspaper costs Rs 5-10 and breakfast for 2 with coffee can come to as little as Rs 50 in a basic 'hotel', but if you intend to eat banana pancakes or pasta backpacker restaurant, you can expect to pay more like Rs 150 a plate.

**Banks** are open Mon-Fri 1030-1430, Sat 1030-1230. Top hotels sometimes have a 24-hr money changing service. **Government offices** open Mon-Fri 0930-1700, Sat 0930-1300 (some open on alternate Sat only). **Post offices** open Mon-Fri 1000-1700, often shutting for lunch, and Sat mornings. **Shops** open Mon-Sat 0930-1800. Bazars keep longer hours.

## Safety

### Personal security

In general the threats to personal security for travellers in India are remarkably small.

However, incidents of petty theft and violence directed specifically at tourists have been on the increase so care is necessary in some places, and basic common sense needs to be used with respect to looking after valuables. Follow the same precautions you would when at home. There have been much reported incidents of sexual assault in Delhi, Kolkata and some more rural areas in the past few years. Avoid wandering alone outdoors late at night. During daylight hours be careful in remote places, especially when alone. If you are under threat, scream loudly. Be very cautious before accepting food or drink from casual acquaintances, as it may be drugged.

The left-wing Maoist extremist Naxalites are active in East Central India. They have a long history of conflict with state and national authorities, including attacks on police and government officials. The Naxalites have not specifically targeted Westerners, but have attacked symbolic targets including Western companies. As a general rule, travellers are advised to be vigilant in the lead up to and on days of national significance, such as Republic Day (26 Jan) and Independence Day (15 Aug) as militants have in the past used such occasions to mount attacks.

Following a major explosion on the Delhi to Lahore (Pakistan) train in Feb 2007 and the Mumbai attacks in Nov 2008, increased security has been implemented on many trains and stations. Similar measures at airports may cause delays for passengers so factor this into your timing. Also check your airline's website for up-to-date information on luggage restrictions.

That said, in the great majority of places visited by tourists, violent crime and personal attacks are extremely rare.

### Travel advice

It is better to seek advice from your consulate than from travel agencies. Before you travel you can contact: **British Foreign & Commonwealth Office Travel Advice Unit**, T0845-850 2829 (Pakistan desk T020-7270 2385), www.fco.gov.uk. **US State Department's Bureau of Consular Affairs**, Overseas Citizens Services, Room 4800, Department of State, Washington, DC 20520-4818, USA, T202-647 1488, www.travel.state.gov. **Australian Department of Foreign Affairs Canberra**, Australia, T02-6261 3305, www.smartraveller.gov.au. Canadian official advice is on www.voyage.gc.ca.

### Theft

Theft is not uncommon. It is best to keep money, passports and valuables with you at all times. Don't regard hotel rooms as being automatically safe; even hotel safes don't guarantee secure storage. Use your own padlock in a budget hotel when you go out. Pickpockets and other thieves operate in the big cities. Crowded areas are particularly high risk. Take special care of your belongings when getting on or off public transport.

When travelling by train, especially overnight, lock your luggage to the metal loops under the seat. Most thefts on trains occur in non-a/c sleeper class carriages – particularly on tourist heavy routes. Travelling bags and cases should be made of tough material, and external pockets (both on bags and on clothing) should never be used for carrying either money or important documents. Strong locks for travelling cases are invaluable, and a leather strap around a case gives extra security. Some travellers prefer to reserve upper berths, which offer some added protection against theft and also the benefit of allowing daytime sleeping. If you put your bags on the upper berth during the day, beware of fellow passengers climbing up for a 'sleep'.

If you have items stolen, they should be reported to the police as soon as possible. Keep a separate record of vital documents, including photocopies of your passport.

Larger hotels will be able to assist in contacting and dealing with the police. Dealings with the police can be very difficult and, in the worst regions, even dangerous. The paperwork involved in reporting losses can be time consuming and irritating and your own documentation (eg passport and visas) may be demanded.

In some states the police occasionally demand bribes, though you should not assume that if procedures move slowly you are automatically being expected to offer a bribe. If you have to go to a police station, try to take someone with you.

If you face really serious problems (eg in connection with a driving accident), contact your consular office as quickly as possible. You should ensure you always have your international driving licence and motorbike or car documentation with you.

Confidence tricksters are particularly common where people are on the move, notably around railway stations or places where budget tourists gather. A common plea is some sudden and desperate calamity; sometimes a letter will be produced in English to back up the claim. The demands are likely to increase sharply if sympathy is shown.

## Telephone

*The international code for India is +91.*

### Mobile phones

Practically all business in India is now conducted via mobile phone. Calls and mobile data are incredibly cheap by global standards – local calls cost as little as half a rupee per min – and if you're in the country for more than a couple of weeks and need to keep in touch it can definitely be worth the hassle to get a local SIM card. Arguably the best service is provided by the government carrier **BSNL/MTNL** but connecting to the service is virtually impossible for foreigners.

Private companies such as **Airtel**, **Vodafone**, **Idea** and **Tata Indicom** are easier to sign up with, but the deals they offer can be befuddling and are frequently changed. To get the connection you'll need to complete a form, have a local address or receipt showing the address of your hotel, and present photocopies of your passport and visa plus 2 passport photos to an authorized reseller – most phone dealers will be able to help, and can also sell top-up. **Univercell**, www.univercell.in, and **The Mobile Store**, www.themobilestore.in, are widespread and efficient chains selling phones and SIM cards.

India is divided into a number of 'calling circles' or regions, and if you travel outside the region where your connection is based (eg. from Kolkata into Darjeeling district), you will pay higher 'roaming' charges for making and receiving calls, and any problems that may occur – with 'unverified' documents, for example – can be much harder to resolve.

### Landlines

You can still find privately run phone booths, usually labelled on yellow boards with the letters 'PCO-STD-ISD'. You dial the call yourself, and the time and cost are displayed on a computer screen. Cheap rate is from 2100-0600. Telephone calls from hotels are usually more expensive (check price before calling), though some will allow local calls free of charge.

A double ring repeated regularly means it is ringing; equal tones with equal pauses means engaged (similar to the UK). If calling a mobile, you're as likely to hear devotional Hindu music or Bollywood hits coming back down the line as a standard ringtone.

One disadvantage of India's tremendous rate of growth is that millions of telephone numbers go out of date every year. Current telephone directories themselves are often out of date and some of the numbers given in this book will have been changed even as we go to press. **Directory enquiries**, T197, can be helpful but works only for the local area code.

## Time

India doesn't change its clocks, so from the last Sun in Oct to the last Sun in Mar the time is GMT +5½ hrs, and the rest of the year it's +4½ hrs (USA, EST +10½ and +9½ hrs; Australia, EST -5½ and -4½ hrs).

## Tipping

A tip of Rs 10 to a bellboy carrying luggage in a modest hotel (Rs 20 in a higher category) would be appropriate. In upmarket restaurants, a 10% tip is acceptable when service is not already included, while in places serving very cheap meals, round off the bill with small change. Indians don't normally tip taxi drivers but a small extra is welcomed. Porters at airports and railway stations often have a fixed rate displayed but will usually press for more. Ask fellow passengers what a fair rate is.

## Tourist information

There are **Government of India** tourist offices in Kolkata and larger towns, as well as West Bengal state tourist offices (sometimes **Tourism Development Corporations**) in the major towns and places of tourist interest. They produce their own tourist literature, either free or sold at a nominal price, and some also have lists of city hotels and paying guest options. The quality of material is improving though maps are often poor. Many offer tours of the city, neighbouring sights and overnight and regional packages. Some run modest hotels and midway motels with restaurants and may also arrange car hire and guides. The staff in the regional and local offices are usually helpful.

## Tour operators

### UK

**Colours Of India**, T020-8347 4020, www.partnershiptravel.co.uk. Tailor-made cultural, adventure, spa and cooking tours.
**Cox & Kings**, T020-7873 5000, www.coxandkings.co.uk. Offer high-quality group tours, private journeys and tailor-made holidays to many of India's regions, from the lavish to the adventurous, planned by experts.
**Dragoman**, T01728-861133, www.dragoman.com. Overland, adventure, camping.
**Exodus**, T0845-287 7408, www.exodus.co.uk. Small group overland and trekking tours.
**Greaves Tours**, T020-7487 9111, www.greavesindia.com. Luxury, tailor-made tours using only scheduled flights. Traditional travel such as road and rail preferred to flights between major cities.
**Master Travel**, T020-7501 6741, www.mastertravel.co.uk. Organizes professional study tours in fields including education and healthcare.
**Pettitts**, T01892-515966, www.pettitts.co.uk. Unusual locations.
**STA Travel**, T0333-321 0099, www.statravel.co.uk. Student and young persons' travel agent.
**Steppes Travel**, T01285-787557, www.steppestravel.co.uk. Wildlife safaris, tiger study tours and cultural tours with strong conservation ethic.
**Trans Indus**, T0844 879 3960, www.transindus.com. Upmarket India travel specialists offering tailor-made and group tours and holidays.

### Continental Europe

**Academische Reizen**, Amsterdam, T020-589 2940, www.academische reizen.nl. All-India group culture tours.
**Chola Voyages**, Paris, T01-4034 5564, www.cholatravels.fr.
**La Maison Des Indes**, Paris, T01-5681 3838, www.maisondes indes.com. Bespoke or group cultural tours.

**Shoestring**, Amsterdam, www.shoestring. com. Group and individual tours.

### India

**Aquaterra Adventures**, T011-2921 2641, www.treknraft.com. Trekking, rafting, kayaking, etc.

**Banyan Tours and Travels**, T0124-456 3800, www.banyantours.com. Pan-Indian operator specializing in bespoke, upmarket travel, with strength in culture, heritage, adventure and wildlife.

**Help Tourism**, Kolkata/Siliguri/Guwahati, T033-2455 0917, www.helptourism.com. Eco-tours in Assam, Arunachal and North Bengal, involving local communities.

**Indebo India**, New Delhi, T011-4716 5500, www.indebo.com. Customized tours and travel-related services throughout India.

**Indiabeat**, B-4 Vijay Path, Tilak Nagar, Jaipur, T0141-651 9797, www.indiabeat. co.uk. Specializing in dream trips and once-in-a-lifetime experiences, this British team decamped to Jaipur have great insider knowledge and insight into India.

**Paradise Holidays**, New Delhi, T011-4552 0735, www.paradiseholidays.com. Wide range of tailor-made tours, from cultural to wildlife.

**Purvi Discovery**, T0373-230 1120, www.purvi web.com. Experienced in tours to Arunachal, Assam and other northeast destinations. A quality outfit with quality accommodation.

**Royal Expeditions**, New Delhi, T011-2623 8545, www.royalexpeditions.com. Specialist staff for customized trips, knowledgeable about options for senior travellers. Owns luxury 4WD vehicles for escorted self-drive adventures in the Himalaya.

**Shanti Travel**, T011-4607 7800, www. shantitravel.com. Tailor-made tours throughout India.

### North America

**Greaves Tours**, T1-800-318 7801. See under UK entry, above.

**Myths and Mountains**, T1-800-670 6984, www.mythsandmountains.com. Culture, crafts and religion.

### Australia and New Zealand

**Adventure World**, T1300-295049, www. adventureworld.co.au. Independent tour operator; also in Auckland, T+64-9524 5118, www.adventureworld.co.nz.

**India Unbound**, T1300-889513, www.india unbound.com.au. Intriguing range of small-group trips and bespoke private tours.

## Visas and immigration

Virtually all foreign nationals, including children, require a visa to enter India. The rules regarding visas change frequently and arrangements for application and collection also vary from town to town so it is essential to check details and costs with the relevant embassy or consulate. These remain closed on Indian national holidays.

As of 2015 India has brought 113 countries into its visa-on-arrival scheme, which after several bizarre false starts is – at time of writing – almost as simple as it sounds. An "e-Visa" costs US$60 and is valid for a stay of up to 30 days; the visa cannot be extended, and only permits travel for tourism purposes. Apply at www.indianvisaonline.gov.in, no later than 4 days before your arrival. For up-to-date information on visa requirements visit www.india-visa.com.

No foreigner needs to register within the 180-day period of their tourist visa. If you have a 1-year visa or as a US citizen a 10-year visa and wish to stay longer than 180 days you will need to register with the Foreign Registration Office. Currently the following visa rules apply:

**Transit** For passengers en route to another country (no more than 72 hrs in India).

**Tourist** Normally valid for 3-6 months from date of issue, though some nationalities may be granted visas for up to 5 years. Multiple entries permitted, but a new rule requires a 2-month wait before you can return to India. The rule doesn't apply if you plan to visit neighbouring countries as part of your trip (eg Nepal, Sri Lanka), but you need clear documentation proving your itinerary.

**5 year** For those of Indian origin, who have held Indian passports.

**Student** Valid up to 1 year from the date of issue. Attach a letter of acceptance from an Indian institution and an AIDS test certificate. Allow up to 3 months for approval.

**Visa extensions** Applications should be made to the Foreigners' Regional Registration Office in Kolkata, or an office of the Superintendent of Police in the District Headquarters, but in reality extensions are rarely granted. After 6 months, you must leave India and apply for a new visa – usually from your home country. For up-to-date information on visa requirements visit www.india-visa.com.

## Weights and measures

Metric is in universal use in the cities. In remote areas local measures are sometimes used. One lakh is 100,000 and 1 crore is 10 million.

## Women travellers

Independent travel is still largely unheard of for Indian women. Although it is relatively safe for women to travel around India, most people find it an advantage to travel with a companion. Even then, privacy is rarely respected and there can be a lot of hassle, pressure and intrusion on your personal space, as well as some outright harassment. Backpackers setting out alone often meet like-minded travelling companions at budget hotels. Cautious women travellers recommend wearing wedding rings, but the most important measure to ensure respect is to dress appropriately, in loose-fitting, non-see-through clothes, covering shoulders, arms and legs (such as a *salwaar kameez*, which can be bought ready-made in Kolkata). Take advantage, too, of the gender segregation on public transport, to avoid hassle and to talk to local women. In mosques women should be covered from head to ankle. **Independent Traveller**, www.independenttraveller.com, runs women-only tours to India.

'Eve teasing', the euphemism for physical harassment, is an unfortunate result of the sexual repression latent in Indian culture, combined with a young male population whose only access to sex education is via the dingy cybercafés. Unaccompanied women are most vulnerable in major cities, crowded bazars and tourist centres where men may follow them and touch them; festival nights are particularly bad for this. Women have reported that they have been molested while being measured for clothing in tailors' shops. If you are harassed, it can be effective to make a scene. Be firm and clear if you don't wish to speak to someone. The best response to staring, whether lascivious or curious, is to avert your eyes down and away. This is not the submissive gesture it might seem, but an effective tool to communicate that you have no interest in any further interaction. Aggressively staring back or confronting the starer can be construed as a come-on. It is best to be accompanied at night, especially when travelling by rickshaw or taxi in towns. Be prepared to raise an alarm if anything unpleasant threatens.

Most railway booking offices have separate women's ticket queues or ask women to go to the head of the general queue. Take advantage, too, of the gender segregation on public transport, to avoid hassle and to talk to local women. All of Kolkata's metro trains have a carriage reserved for women, and some buses have seats reserved for women at the front.

# Index *Entries in bold refer to maps*

# Credits

**Footprint credits**

**Editor**: Nicola Gibbs
**Production and layout**: Emma Bryers
**Maps**: Kevin Feeney
**Colour section**: Patrick Dawson

**Publisher**: Felicity Laughton
Patrick Dawson
**Marketing**: Kirsty Holmes
**Sales**: Diane McEntee
**Advertising and content partnerships**:
Debbie Wylde

**Photography credits**

**Front cover**: neelsky/Shutterstock.com
**Back cover top**: Seree Tansrisawat/
Shutterstock.com
**Back cover bottom**: Debasis Das/
Shutterstock.com.
**Inside front cover**: neelsky/Shutterstock.
com, Ian Taylor/SuperStock.com, Luciano
Mortula/Shutterstock.com.

**Colour section**
**Page 1**: Rudra Narayan Mitra/
Shutterstock.com.
**Page 2**: Eye Ubiquitous/SuperStock.com.
**Page 4**: neelsky/Shutterstock.com,
Alvaro Leiva/SuperStock.com.
**Page 5**: neelsky/Shutterstock.com,
Aldo Pavan/SuperStock.com.
**Page 6**: Mahantesh C Morabad/
Shutterstock.com.
**Page 7**: David Evison/Shutterstock.com,
Photononstop/SuperStock.
**Page 8**: Tawin Mukdharakosa/
Shutterstock.com.

**Duotone**
**Page 24**: Attila JANDI/Shutterstock.com.

Printed in Spain by GraphyCems

**Publishing information**
Footprint Kolkata & West Bengal
3rd edition
© Footprint Handbooks Ltd
June 2016

ISBN: 978 1 910120 87 3
CIP DATA: A catalogue record for this book
is available from the British Library

® Footprint Handbooks and the
Footprint mark are a registered
trademark of Footprint Handbooks Ltd

Published by Footprint
6 Riverside Court
Lower Bristol Road
Bath BA2 3DZ, UK
T +44 (0)1225 469141
F +44 (0)1225 469461
footprinttravelguides.com

Distributed in the USA by
National Book Network, Inc.

Every effort has been made to ensure that
the facts in this guidebook are accurate.
However, travellers should still obtain advice
from consulates, airlines, etc about travel
and visa requirements before travelling.
The authors and publishers cannot
accept responsibility for any loss, injury
or inconvenience however caused.